THE PE'

Rugby League fans say "Enough is Enough"

Written and Compiled by Ray Gent

With contributions from Allan Reeve, Matt Anniss,
Tim Wilkinson, Peter Roe, Gloryhunter,
Harry Edgar, Lord Hoyle of Warrington,
John Grime, Terry Wynn MEP, Roger Grime,
Alex Service, Phil Stockton, Dave Hadfield, HaloMan
and many others from the Rugby League family

Front cover design by Stuart Gent

Illustrations by Karen Pownall, Stuart Gent and Glyn Wall

The Parrs Wood Press
<u>MANCHESTER</u>

First Published 2002

THE PARRS WOOD PRESS
St Wilfrid's Enterprise Centre
Royce Road, Manchester, M15 5BJ
www.parrswoodpress.com

© Ray Gent 2002

ISBN: 1 903158 26 5

This book was produced by The Parrs Wood Press
and Printed in Great Britain by:

MFP Design and Print
Longford Trading Estate
Thomas Street
Stretford
Manchester M32 0JT

CONTENTS

ACKNOWLEDGEMENTS

THANKS TO:

David Hinchliffe, MP for Wakefield
The All-Party Parliamentary Rugby League Group
The contributors and illustrators
League Express publications
Rugby Leaguer
Local newspapers and radio as mentioned in the appendices
The Parrs Wood Press
Various internet sites and message boards
The Petition was supported by silkstream and auvergne seasons,
which can be found at
www.silkstream.com and www.auvergneseasons.com
The volunteers and 30,000 plus signatories

INTRODUCTION

"Yours in Sport"

The phrase above requires some microscopic examination. Sport can be defined as fun, enjoyable, rousing, passionate, exhilarating, refreshing, dramatic, serious, and, at times, touched with sadness or tragedy.

Rugby league is all of these but the emotion that has come over most clearly in the course of the petition has been the fans' deep frustration with the way certain media outlets present their sport and the inefficiency of those who run it.

The genuine rugby league supporter, hundreds of whom have contributed to the petition's success, thousands if each signatory is counted as a contributor, is truly a torchbearer for the game.

No doubt there have been many searching questions asked throughout league's chequered history regarding the media's attitude towards our game, alas very few satisfactory answers. Yet the sport's governing bodies are not without blame. Most ordinary fans of rugby league are of the same opinion that their game has been like a ship without a rudder over the last few years. Several contributors will confirm this, as you explore the book's content. This rudderless ship may as well have been floundering in the fog, lost far out in the deepest oceans. Without the influence of a captain at the helm to take the game into clearer weather, it has struggled to move on. Political in-fighting, no clear vision of where the game is going, no strength in leadership, nor a sense of all for one and one for all.

We have Super League who run the top twelve professional teams, the Rugby Football League administering the clubs in the Northern

Ford Premiership, BARLA in charge of the amateurs and many other controlling bodies. Add some politics and self-interest into the cooking pot, and you come up with an unsavoury dish.

Yet rugby league can stand tall and proud with the best in sport. Its one hundred plus years are steeped in dramatic moments and achievement, especially in the face of adversity. Rugby league has never been afraid of change, change that other sports later imitate. Very few can argue that their game has had to endure the treacherous attacks that rugby league has had to go through.

Is it sport for certain media outlets to continue spitting venom at the sport?

Even though it does shoot itself in the foot on occasions and seems to take a perverse delight in continually jumping through blazing hoops, it is still a vibrant game. Our game. The petition was the fans' way of striking back. We, the "little people" in every city, town and village, defend our birthright tenaciously.

Rugby league has been an integral part of my life for over thirty-five years, and my son, Stuart, will doubtless carry on the family tradition. The rugby league family is like that and no matter the political weather, we, the fans, are proud people. No one will be allowed to trample on our game, hence the petition for fair play.

Of course, there is criticism in this book of the way the game of rugby league has been governed; this is not to detract from the many decent people who work with vigour for the sport within the various organisations in so many capacities, often unrecognised. Likewise, there are also some decent national journalists who try hard to give league a fair crack in the face of extreme adversity. But the overriding feeling is that we are being cheated.

Whether you agree with the book's content or not, it should give rise to some healthy debate.

THE PETITION

Allan Reeve was instrumental in obtaining around 11,000 of the petition signatures with the help of his good wife Jacky, their son Arron and friend Anthony. Let Allan start the ball rolling with a trip back in time, as well as his views on events, after which the petition unfolds....

Why Are They Attacking This 'Great Game'?

I have been watching this great game of rugby league for over forty years since my father and my uncle Bill started taking me as a mere four year old. Wigan's my team, having watched them through thick and thin.

My first memories were of getting off the bus near Wigan Little Theatre and walking alongside the River Douglas. There was a hustle and bustle of men, many wearing big coats to keep the chill out with not a few of them sporting flat caps or trilbies. The sound of the sellers, who used to shout out 'programme, programme', in those days added to the hubbub and enhanced the atmosphere. We used to pass by the dressing rooms where the wonderful aroma of wintergreen filled the air. I was smitten immediately and this was before we had even got on the ground. The anticipation was no less walking up to Knowsley Road or over Bridge Foot to Wilderspool, the atmosphere was absolutely addictive.

I was lucky in that I was around to idolise Billy Boston (I almost said the likes of Billy Boston but there was no one like him in my opinion) and cheer as he went the length of the field leaving a trail of players in his wake on his way under the sticks. The first player to stick in my conscious mind however was not Billy B. but Bill Sayer or "Soz" - Wigan`s hooker at that time. Maybe because he was always in the middle of the big props going into a scrum or at acting half-back but I think it was because of his craggy, disjointed rugby features. Still, he didn`t frighten me, he was one of ours.

It was a wonderful world and as I got older I began to enjoy the intrinsic pleasures of the game. They used to lift me over the turn-

3

stile in those days but they've had their money back a thousand-fold since and I begrudge them not a penny of it for the pleasure this great game has given to me and millions of others. Great players over the years include: Alex Murphy, Ellery Hanley, Clive Sullivan, Peter Sterling, Mal Meninga, Neil Fox, Brian Glover of Warrington, Trevor Foster, Harold Poynton of Wakefield in the Rocky Turner era, Hardisty and Hepworth of Castleford, Offiah, Lewis Jones, Gus Risman, Harold Wagstaffe, Jack Wilkinson of Halifax, Shaun Edwards and many, many more. The list is endless, and all have enriched the game of rugby league and have given me, and so many others, fond memories. Some of them have broken my heart but I forgive them. My philosophy, one I have always tried to impart to my children, is that you only hate the opposition for eighty minutes but after that you're all part of the same fraternity.

Over the years I`ve seen many changes in rugby league, most have ultimately improved the quality of the game in the long run such as the four tackle and then six tackle rules. They were radical changes when they were introduced, ultimately speeding up the game but were not universally welcomed at the time. The tap penalty re-start, introduced in 1966, cut down the number of scrums and in doing also speeded up the action.

Rugby league has never been afraid to adopt new ideas, as mentioned by Ray previously, proved in 1906 by reducing the number of players per side from 15 to 13, and ultimately it has evolved over the years into a spectacular contest between absolutely world class athletes.

As far as I know the sport of rugby league has done nothing to attack any other sport with a view to destroying it. Bearing this in mind, the world was going along swimmingly just before the start of Super League IV season when I had a shock whilst listening to Radio Five. The campaign for the launch had, I think, been devised by Super League themselves and Leeds-based advertising agency CWG and involved a tongue-in-cheek cinema and billboard hoarding advertisements which depicted some Super League players in the shower posing the question, "How was it for you?"

The panel discussing it totally ripped the sport apart, not just the campaign, which many saw as harmless fun, but the sport itself. There were remarks such as 'They would, wouldn't they'. They really ripped into the game and totally belittled the sport. Now that, in itself, may not seem to be earth-shattering and Super League did get some positive feedback from it when it was featured on Channel 4, but to me it signalled a new tone in presenting rugby league as an "out group". It became fashionable amongst certain individuals in the media to denigrate the sport at every opportunity

We all know that there have been many mistakes made in the administration of rugby league over the years, but when our own people are doing their dirty washing in the open it legitimises any snipes made at the game by people who like nothing better than to see the demise of one of the most fabulous sports in the world. Who are these people and what motivates them to denigrate and attempt to assassinate rugby league? Well, to answer that we have to go back a long way. There is considerable contempt for each other from both sides of the rugby divide. Many people who follow rugby league think there is nothing more boring than watching a series of set pieces and endless kicks and penalties with little or no attacking flow. They tune in to see what all the hype is about and think they have got the test card not a Test match. Rugby union types, and there are genuine union types, think of league, and again I've heard this mentioned a number of times on national radio, as a load of fellows running about 'up there'. 'Up there' - that about sums up the difference. It's about the so-called north - south divide and we are not allowed to be better at anything than those down south.

As I said, you have to go back a long way to find out the root of why the game of rugby league is being attacked in the media from outside the game as no other sport has ever been. Both codes have a common history. In 1823 William Webb Ellis famously and allegedly first picked up the ball and ran with it. Forty-eight years later came the formation of the Rugby Football Union and the notion of running with the ball reverted to pick the ball up and kick it once more. Throw in a version of the Eton Wall game to keep the big fellows who can't run happy, and an exclusive new gentleman's club to run the game was born for the well-to-do, better-nourished classes. The common, less well-fed people could play Association or Soccer Football. Up north, however, things had already got under way a full year before Yorkshire entertained Lancashire in the first ever representative county game.

The formation of the RFU, on 26th January 1871, consisted entirely of 32 London and suburban clubs at a meeting at the Pall Mall Restaurant in Regent Street. The likes of King's College, Richmond Civil Service, Guy's Hospital, Law and Wellington College were founder members of the embryonic organisation. Of those 32 original sides, only Harlequins remain in the top flight today. Gradually, the organisation spread out of the capital and clubs were allowed to be associated from other areas.

It was not too long before Yorkshire and Lancashire started to dominate both county and club competitions whilst supplying the national team with the bulk of its best players. Many of the players down south were in salaried positions whilst those up north tended to be in hourly paid occupations and Saturday morning, in those days, was part of the regular working week. Obviously, in sport, if you are successful you are going to travel further afield to take part in meaningful competition and to the players in the Northern Counties that meant loss of earnings which they could ill afford.

The broken time payment argument simmered for a number of years, as did the argument of the owners of the Northern clubs about the venue of the AGM. They argued that as they were more successful than their southern counterparts the AGM, if not taken up north permanently, should at least be alternated. In all, twenty Northern clubs broke away to form the Northern Union in 1895 and there was a lot of bad blood between the two ruling factions, which many think has never gone away.

Until only the last few years, when union went professional, any player who dared to play even the lowest level of amateur rugby league, if found out, could never play the fifteen-a-side code again. That just shows the bitterness that existed, and probably still does, in some quarters. The fact that many amateur rugby union players through the history of the game have, because they were good at what they did on a rugby field, decided to go professional and exploit their talents did nothing to endear the league code to its estranged sibling.

David Watkins' treatment by the powers-that-be at Cardiff Arms Park is a good example of the disgraceful ostracism endured by former rugby union players who dared to go professional. David was a great fly half for Wales in the late sixties, helping them to triple crowns in 63, 64 and 65. He also captained the British Lions so he had paid his dues. He was one of the first players, in fact the first that I saw, who kicked place kicks 'around the corner' using his instep which is common practice these days but at that time kickers used a straight run up and toe ended the ball. He still holds the record for scoring in the most consecutive club games, for Salford in the1972/3 and1973/4 seasons, contributing 41 tries and 403 goals in 92 games. His reward for going professional was being refused entry at Cardiff Arms Park to watch an international. He was picked out of a 60,000 plus crowd and turned away.

Now imagine the converse situation with Jason Robinson, Henry Paul and Iestyn Harris. As far as I know, apart from a few mindless individuals, no one has wished the three prominent cross-coders anything but well in their new careers (all three have recently transferred from league to union). The difference between their case and that of David Watkins is that he was picked up by Salford chairman Brian Snape purely to make the team a better one and not to knock the other code.

THE PETITION

Take Jason. He, like Henry Paul, has achieved almost everything in league apart from a series win against the Kangaroos. Robinson did play in the 1993 series against NZ - 3-0 to GB. However, a distortion of the facts and time-scale by one tabloid would have you believing that, had he not found God and turned to union when he did, probably both in the same weekend, he would still be throwing down twenty pints a night and running amok around town.

In Henry Paul's case, the depiction offered in a middle-ground newspaper was that he used to have his wages subsidised by the fruit machines in Wakefield's social club, a practice commonplace on a much bigger scale in Australia. However, to compare that with `the opulence of a Mayfair Hotel, a metaphor for his new life ahead, is not comparing like with like and is described purely to denigrate rugby league. For goodness sake someone, throw me a whippet! What about the big fat opulent cheques that came after that at Wigan and Bradford?

Iestyn Harris was an extremely talented individual but, in league, as yet still with unfulfilled potential and yet he was described in the media as the single most important player in the rugby league ranks and the signal of the end. I think not. Three players, or at least three mainstream players have crossed over, whilst Robinson and Henry could quite have easily gone to NRL in Australia and would have been lost to the British League scene anyway. That is hardly an exodus from the game that the media would have us all to believe. Thank goodness that Kieron Cunningham and Kris Radlinski stood up and were counted by remaining loyal to league.

I don't think that the bitterness against league has declined and some people who pull strings have got Pinocchio, Muffin the Mule and all the Flower-Pot Men dancing for them in some of the sports pages.

Even before the petition started, I began to notice other dribbles of criticism against rugby league appearing in features and articles, which were obviously meant to belittle the game. An example occurred during the radio commentary on a football match on a quagmire of a pitch. The picture painted was of a dour, tedious affair with players slipping and sliding all over the place. One of the commentators compared it to a rugby league match. His co-presenter corrected him with the quip that it couldn't be as there was a crowd on the ground. Another was when I heard Geoff Capes, in response to a question from Nickki Campbell of Radio Five as to which code of rugby he preferred, say that he understood that rugby league was finishing. Not for one minute do I believe that Geoff was being facetious, nor had he any axe to grind about rugby league, but that was his honest perception of the situation as represented to him and millions of other people in this country.

I was beginning to believe it myself when, one day, wife Jacky, ten year old son Aaron and I were waiting for the start of a match at Knowsley Road between Saints and Wigan, a game attended by something in the region of 15,000 people, televised by Sky and eventually won by Saints. A gentleman approached us on the terracing with a clipboard and asked us if we would sign a petition regarding the mistreatment currently being handed out to rugby league by the media. That gentleman was Ray Gent, a lover of the game and a Saints fan. Not only did we sign the petition but also we offered to help him in a cause we whole-heartedly believed in. It was in my mind that we would go round a few friends, family and parents at the rugby club that Aaron plays for, Burtonwood Bulldogs.

Before I go any further I would just like to mention the Bulldogs as an example. Burtonwood is only a small village and in 1998 a group of parents got together and formed an under eights team under the guidance of head coach and chairman Wayne Tapper. Wayne is as Welsh as you like and comes from a union background and even though there is a rugby union club in the village, he was so smitten with the league game that he took it up in preference. The two clubs sit side by side quite happily on adjacent pitches - and that's how it should be. The point is that from that one under eights team it has developed into four age groups and eventually, as the bottom set is replaced each year by a new set of lads and the other groups move up, it will have every age group from eight to open age. That's just one example and the lads really want to play. Now that's not the dying game you are be led to believe.

My extrapolations may sound like paranoia of a conspiracy theory but as Ronald Regan is credited with saying, when he was fully compos mentis, that just because you're paranoid still doesn't mean they are **not** out to get you!

Back to Ray. On speaking to him I was taken aback when he told me he was hoping to get over ten thousand signatures and that he had already been in touch with David Hinchliffe, MP for Wakefield, to present the petition when it was completed. I thought that he was being a bit optimistic but I underestimated the strength of feeling people had about the way rugby league is being hammered in the media for people were queuing up to sign. Personally, I would have worded the petition's legend a bit more strongly but the message is the same.

To some people, a petition is not the way to go about things, but how else could the ordinary fans have their say? And have their say to the tune of 30,000 protests about the way our game is being denigrated in the media. On the terraces of Leeds, Bradford, Salford, Wigan, Warrington St. Helens, Widnes, Huddersfield, Halifax, Hull, Castleford, Wakefield, London, Wrexham and several Northern Ford Clubs, fans have spoken as one. People from areas such as Scarborough, Birmingham, Northern Ireland, South Wales, Edinburgh, Lincoln, Douglas, Sunderland, Liverpool, Cumbria, the Wirral, London and many more areas who care about and enjoy the greatest game have echoed their views. The chorus is, **'Enough is Enough'**

1

"And now for a game that no one cares about... Rugby League."

This sweeping statement began an article in the "Daily Express" shortly after the 2000 Rugby League World Cup Final. It was a full page spread shot through with mischief and venom, the journalist concerned akin to a vulture fighting for its share of the so-called corpse.

Copies of the said article were sent to all twelve Super League clubs, the Rugby Football League and the Rugby League Parliamentary Group of MP's. A letter of complaint was also enclosed. Only Lord Hoyle of Warrington replied. This was my first taste of apathy within the game. (N.B. Lord Hoyle later confirmed that this article had been sent to the Press Complaints Commission)

There is no doubt that the World Cup tournament was poorly arranged. An event that depends on a bandwagon effect needs to start with a bang to achieve public profile. With the opening match (England versus Australia) an evening kick off to accommodate Sky's football results service, this was always going to be a struggle. It all seemed to be fair play at the start, as the media men got on with the task of telling all and sundry that the competition would make a profit in the order of £3m, huge in RL terms. One organizer even had a diary of events in a weekly league publication.

However, other media vultures were lurking in the background, as shown by the odd sly comment in a few papers. It was as if some media were just waiting for everything to go pear-shaped. Still, the outlook remained positive.

* Sign online comment refers to messages gathered from the internet version of the petition, which attracted worldwide contributions.

SIGN ONLINE COMMENT
(fan in Townsville, Australia)

"The people will choose."

Cloudy Skies Beckon

The first sign of stormy clouds came with the announcement that the American owners of Lincoln Financial Group were going to pull the plug on their UK set up. Lincoln had come forward as the main sponsors of the event, and so this news came as quite a shock. Immediately, the 'enemy' took this up, and used it as the first real attack, although Lincoln assured the game that the sponsorship was safe.

Another major contributor to any problems was to commence the competition in the afternoon with the Ireland versus Samoa match at Windsor Park in Belfast, rather than the game between England and Australia, which was played at a cold, wet Twickenham, home of the Rugby Football Union, in the early evening.

With the Ireland match only producing a small, if enthusiastic, crowd it did not go down well on BBC TV. In fact, the BBC commentator, Steve Ryder, had his first snipe at the game when the television pictures switched from Ireland over to Scotland where a union international was taking place. In his own words: "I see that you have the marketing right, as the stadium is filling up nicely." Ticketmaster had been misinforming fans that the match was sold out at 15,000, when in fact only 3,200 fans eventually turned up. It is now common knowledge that the RFL's subcontracted ticket agency, Ticketmaster, advised many callers that various games were sold out when the truth was that they had simply sold their allocation. Twickenham and Windsor Park were two such instances.

Crowds were disappointing for many reasons, not least the low-key marketing, ticket agency ineptitude and monsoon weather. It had been the wettest autumn for many a year, in fact the wettest October since records began. An evening game at Widnes witnessed fans having to queue up for tickets due to no turnstiles being open. Two elderly gentlemen were trying their level best to cope in one small, unlit box whilst hundreds of fans were stranded in the twilight zone, patiently waiting to get into the stadium. Many eventually just gave up and went home. Such events typified what was the first-ever 16 team RL World Cup.

Use of the 'grandparent' qualification rule helped supplement local talent of smaller countries, mainly with Australasians, to enable them to take part at a reasonable level of competitiveness and safety. Sure enough, media attention focussed on this aspect and the competition denigrated as if the whole competition was Australian.

The team from Lebanon qualified for the competition by playing three games against Italy, Morocco and USA, causing unprecedented scenes in Lebanon. Their coach, John Elias, played despite being stricken with cancer. Such positive stories, however, went unreported as the team was generally derided as 'second rate Australians'. In fact, nine of the Cedars were born at home, the others being largely 'second generation' but all plying their trade in the Sydney Metropolitan Cup competition. An easy mistake for an uninformed journalist with an axe to grind.

Packed houses in France, a 30-odd year crowd record in Wales (which could have been many more only for the ticket cock-up) and a national holiday being declared in Papua New Guinea so that 10,000 people could welcome their team home, were all stories lost on 'Fleet Street'.

Footnote

During the Sky TV broadcast featuring the petition (mentioned later in the book), there was a comment by Greg McCallum of the Rugby Football League that gave food for thought. It was suggested that there was possibly a concerted effort by certain influences to try and derail the tournament. This was never quantified, and so left one with no answers as to what was behind the statement.

The above may seem an insane way to start the book because it gives the media the excuse to say they were right. However, unlike with some journalists, the truth and facts can be faced when it matters. The point is that such reporting was way over the top and shot full of sarcasm. It appeared to be written with a very large smirk.

QUOTE FROM THE SAINTS MESSAGE BOARD
(XYZ comments)

"Dedication is needed to take our game forward."

The Sniping Gathers Momentum

After the World Cup, matters then settled down due to the Super League season being finished. There is never much media space given to league over winter, even though the Northern Ford Premier clubs play. As a matter of fact, it is sometimes hard to find coverage in the Super League season itself.

THE PETITION

THE PETITION

The next major event was the Rugby League Challenge Cup Final between St. Helens and Bradford, to be held once again at Twickenham, the home of the Rugby Football Union. It was as if rugby league was jinxed at this venue for the weather was atrocious once again. The Saints contingent did not have the luck of the draw regarding ends, many huddled in the end that was only half covered - and on a bitterly cold, wet day, it seemed so very inhospitable. Nature scorned the event as the heavens opened up just before kick off, and tens of thousands endured an elemental soaking. The game, although not a classic, was still tense, but wasn't it a pleasure just to get home to a hot cup of tea!

Now for the first real insult of the year. The "Sunday Express" published a scathing attack on the game the next day. The headline started with: "League thrown to the Lions." It suggested the inter-code battle was won and the hundred-year war over. Rugby union, for so long snootily contemptuous of its cloth-capped provincial cousins in rugby league, had finally overwhelmed the ancient foe. (The only thing is, there is no recollection of league fans raising the white flag). The evidence had been littered all over a defining season in the history of the handling game.

The article went on to mention that the Rugby League World Cup the previous autumn was shambolic. England was quickly obliterated, having been forced to play without their superstar Jason Robinson, because he had been lured away by a £1 million union contract. Is this the same player that union pundits said would not make the grade in his new code of rugby?

It stated that crowds were often meagre, whilst TV figures were derisory (a claim at odds with BBC's own viewing figures). Comment was made that no one really cared about the tournament, no matter how hard it was hyped. Praise was given to the rugby union game (no change here) and the thread of the article was to downgrade rugby league.

The most damning piece was reference to "Now the rats have

become Lions", a reference to Jason Robinson changing codes, and to an old quote from bygone days when league was referred to by some in the establishment as 'rats in a sewer'.

Further on, it asked who cares that he is a convert from the league code? Who cares about the old days of looking down loftily on rugby men who made a hard, dirty living by being paid to play the game? Technically, this is not correct. Players were paid as compensation for lost work time and not as full time professionals. Yet there seems nothing wrong today with regards to union players being paid!

The final paragraph stated that Jason Robinson is the symbol of this new rugby age. He is the Billy Whizz of the 15-man game, the only kind of rugby that matters here anymore. I wonder which part of the nation 'here' is?

SIGN ONLINE COMMENT
(fan in Wakefield)

"The game is here to stay. It's about time people realised it."

The Volcano Erupts

The insulting article caused a reaction in the land of rugby league, akin to mount Etna erupting. At the time, I was still a novice in the strange world of internet message boards, trying desperately to get used to my own club's version.

On Monday morning, all hell let loose.

The Judge (shipping tycoon) started a thread reference to the article. (I always thought a thread was something to do with cotton, but not in my new world of message boards). The news soon reached epidemic proportions and was filling page after page on the message board. A massive e-mail campaign was preached from one and all as the said newspaper was bombarded with salvoes of complaints. Outrage was to the fore; the rugby league band was playing; league troops were marching to the sound of the trumpet. No one dared refer to us as sewer rats, mad mice yes, but not sewer rats! Fans' tolerance levels blew through the roof.

Computers were going up in smoke, such was the counter attack, but there was no time for a lull in the proceedings as the article had to be repulsed. Fans, an ex-player and even a Member of Parliament replied. The furore was confirmed the following Sunday when the paper printed two full pages of letters, probably the only time one can recollect that two full pages in a national newspaper were devoted to rugby league.

When the steam began to evaporate, mention was made of starting a petition to vent our anger at such an unjustified media onslaught. In the heat of the moment, I volunteered to back the clarion call. Sadly, a moment of truth dawned, for there were not too many other fans wishing to get involved.

My life has been littered with marching into uncharted waters and here was a prime example. It isn't easy to retreat from battle once an attack has been declared. Go where others will not tread is the motto. Mix with the sharks and play with the bears. "Am I stupid or what?" And so it was off towards the front line with trumpets still blaring in my ears to start the petition.

Blast from the Past

Petitions are not all new, as I had been party to one some way back in the seventies when, at the time, I belonged to a group called the '1895 Club' based in St. Helens, 1895 being the year when the game of rugby split for broken-time payments. The group was a pro-active organization that had the good of rugby league at heart. The cam-

THE PETITION

paign trail included student rugby league, being allowed to play league in the armed forces and media coverage. There was an actual ban on playing rugby league during my army career, a personal injustice that can never be rectified.

The petition at the time concerned media coverage on the BBC, or the lack of it. Nothing seems to change. Anyway, a few dedicated fans eventually collected 10,000 signatures (no message boards in those days). It was fun going to places like Alt Park in Huyton, Liverpool, on the petition trail. Not big crowds but very friendly. Collecting signatures in the bar after the match was a warm experience.

The petition was going to be handed in at BBC Television House in London the morning of the 1976 Challenge Cup Final between Saints and Widnes. As it was our own beloved Saints in the final, we all decided to travel down early Friday evening and stay for two nights, my first weekend at a cup final.

On the Saturday morning, the Chairman of the group duly handed over the petition in front of several press officers. The press statement read that it was not against Eddie Waring, the then BBC Rugby League commentator, but about media coverage in general. The press release in the Evening Standard that night read: "Fifteen burly rugby league fans hand in petition to the BBC complaining about Eddie Waring." I wouldn't mind but one fan was only eight stone wringing wet!

The events which followed were hilarious. Having won the cup, had a refreshing kip and a shower, it was now time to celebrate. Many fans were assembled in the bar including representatives from Saints, Wigan, Widnes, Leeds and Castleford.

Once the drink had been flowing it was conga time. This huge line of fans dressed in all the colours of the rainbow started out from the bar and proceeded right through to the foyer. This giant foyer had probably seen nothing like it. One large American was heard to say: "Gee whiz Mabel! What have we here?" As the night progressed there was dancing on the tables (sturdy enough for league fans) with a real cowboy atmosphere. The barman was heard to shout: "Don't mind the dancing on the tables, but please bring your glasses back." Surely we never made a spectacle of ourselves?

But I digress from the petition.

QUOTE FROM THE SAINTS MESSAGE BOARD
(Supersaint)

"I have to admit that I was sceptical at first about the petition. Not because I did not believe in it, because I did. I thought that no matter what happens, rugby league wouldn't get the sort of publicity that it deserves. But how wrong was I?"

2

Out with the Clipboard

The front line beckons! It was the first Friday after the Challenge Cup Final and the Saints were playing Leeds at Headingley. Joyous after the cup win, the Saints took support in droves, with a really cracking atmosphere complementing the clear spring evening.

On reaching the ground, it was time to split up from cousin Linda, her daughter Karen and my son Stuart. It was time to lead the cavalry (although there was no one behind in support) with petition board in hand. The first port of call was the bar under the South Stand and then on to the South Stand itself. The Leeds fans were very enthusiastic in wanting to sign the petition.

At half time, the exercise was taken to the Saints supporters gathered at the scoreboard end. All in all it was a successful night with over 200 signatories signing the petition and many fans actually confirming that most coverage in the media was completely derogatory.

SIGN ONLINE COMMENT
(fan in Wigan)

"I'm sorry but you could all be in trouble with the trade descriptions act, calling yourselves national newspapers and media. More like HOME COUNTIES newspaper and media. God forgive me for living in the north!"

As for the Saints it was a disaster. Still wobbly from the celebrations of winning the Challenge Cup, Leeds put over seventy points on them.

One point that stuck in my mind was that several fans had travelled from far and wide. One particular fan that signed the petition had travelled from Scotland. This was to give some food for thought later on and will be explained further in the book.

Move the Goalposts

The journey back home found me deep in thought. The realization struck home like a thunderbolt as to what had been taken on. Therefore there was a quick reassessment from the original target of 10,000 signatories down to 5,000. It was felt there was no way that 10,000 could be achieved without any assistance at that point and I didn't feel like courting embarrassment.

Programme of Events

The next home match for the Saints saw the petition afforded an airing in the Saints programme, no less. Alex Service, the well-known Saints' club historian, had taken the trouble to write an article.

There was mention of the Challenge Cup Final and it read:

"Perhaps, like me, you bought a larger selection of papers than usual on the Sunday after Twickenham. It is a fascinating exercise to compare how the national press cover the Challenge Cup Final. I suppose there was added interest this year with the venue and there were one or two predictable little 'pops' in the direction of rugby league. Over the past few years, however, there have been more 'loose cannons' than normal.

One article, by a bloke called Jim Holden - Chief Sports Correspondent, no less, of the "Sunday Express" - was so full of vitriol and so offensive to rugby league people in general that it caused wholesale anger throughout the 13-a-side

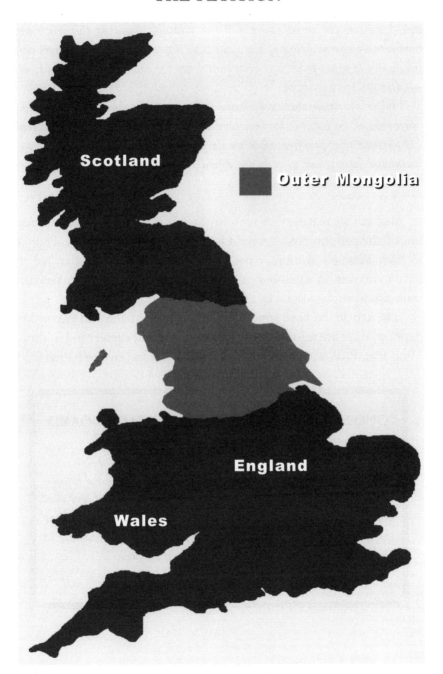

code. I am sure you are all-aware of the unacceptable content of this article and have already informed the paper of your total displeasure. Supporters were only too pleased to sign a petition of complaint before the match at Headingley Leeds - believe me, every bit helps.

Holden's assertion that rugby league is dead and buried could - and should - affect sales of his paper in the heartland areas of our game. That's his problem. Yet we must react positively when we see such biased and un-balanced pieces of journalism against our game in the media. Talk about the north-south divide being alive and well!"

Alex did a great service with his article in that there was no way out of the petition now. It would have to go on until the end. Thanks to Alex must go in more ways than one for confirming that we all have to do our bit when our great game comes under attack. You can walk round rugby league but not over it!

The article did have some bearing on sales of the said paper. My nephew, Russ, mentioned that he was selling 60% fewer in his shop. Mind you, Russ was telling all and sundry not to buy the paper!

QUOTE FROM THE SAINTS MESSAGE BOARD
(Agent Mulder)

"When I started collecting signatures I had to ask people and explain what it was all about. But as it began to take off, I found fans were coming to me to sign and the clipboard would suddenly disappear along a line of fans. It was great to see people from different clubs united in their desire for more publicity and fairness in the press."

THE PETITION

Help Is On Its Way

During the next few matches it was all up hill, as fans were prepared to sign the petition but not get out there and collect signatures themselves. Then, after many failed attempts to muster help, out of the blue came John o' Gaunt (John Dotters).

John had recently started to post messages on the Saints message board and was a new name amongst many others. One day, an e-mail was received from John offering help and encouragement. This was the first sign of a chink in the dark clouds. At last there was someone willing to join the crusade for justice.

Once contact had been made with John, belief in the petition grew. John took it on himself to post messages onto other message boards asking for assistance. This was such a great help, as I was still a technical novice and only just manoeuvring around the Saints message board. A big thanks must go in print to John who has given more help and encouragement than he thinks.

Information was now being placed on different sites for other fans to view developments. Even yours truly managed, after several failures, to get onto other message boards to spread the gospel. Not being an internet buff, it was with great satisfaction finding communication so easy.

Following on from John's helping hand there were a couple of other posts on the Saints message board from fans in Hull. Conboys and ramses had seen the details of the petition and were only too glad to give assistance. This was another breakthrough, as there were now fans over a wider geographical spread helping out. Once again, praise is given to both, including Conboys' wife, Sue, who has never tired of taking on the challenge. This now meant the petition was gaining further momentum.

The funniest thing that happened during the petition concerned Conboys. He had changed ends at half time of a match and during the second half realized that he had left his clipboard behind. Once the match was over he quickly went round to the other end of the ground to retrieve the clipboard. What he was greeted with was amazing. Whilst he had been away, 50 more fans had signed the petition. What dedication for the game!

Conboys (Ste Conboy) had mentioned that he was fed up with media coverage for some time before the petition. He went on to suggest that the marketing could be improved at Super League (Europe) and at the Rugby Football League (Red Hall). He was far from impressed with the World Cup in terms of organisation and finishes with: "We need people who generally care about the game, and are not over eager to jump into bed with union."

SIGN ONLINE COMMENT
(fan from Co. Waterford)

"Journalists like these are very sad people with nothing else to do."

A Major Breakthrough

Possibly the biggest impact on the petition was to come via the first home meeting between Saints and Wigan, although at the time hopes were never high as to what fans would offer in the way of support. That way I wasn't going to feel let down.

Going back to my early days of insurance work, I used to knock on doors for a living. This was done for over ten years with never a night off. Come rain, hail or shine, I would be out canvassing. I have to admit it was a very lonely existence during those long, dark, cold nights.

On average, it used to take 60 knocks on doors before someone would say "yes". That meant 59 people giving a deflating "no". A few people that I trained fell by the wayside, as they were only prepared to knock on 59 doors. This meant that they went away in rejection, never reaching out for that one final knock. So near to the goal, yet so far away.

Now going back to the Saints versus Wigan match, here is a prime example of persistence paying off. I must have spoken to hundreds of fans before Allan Reeve signed the petition. He then went on to explain that he, too, was disillusioned with media coverage and asked could he help. Here I was amongst the Wigan fans and now finding one who wanted to do more. (At this point my target had increased back to over 10,000 petition signatories).

I now take my hat off to Allan, wife Jacky, son Arron and friend Anthony. By early September they had amassed a staggering 10,000 plus signatures. This petition would not have reached its current standing at the time of 22,000 without their contribution. The moral of the story is keep on knocking, as one day someone will say yes. For those who say nothing will ever change, it can only be reiterated that you must keep on knocking at doors.

QUOTE FROM THE SAINTS MESSAGE BOARD
(Blobby Goulding)

"When the idea was mentioned about a petition I was all for it. I didn't know what impact it would make, but it has been massive."

The Highs and Lows of Technology

The petition trail continued with many messages going on the different friendly internet sites across the U.K. Messages were sent out requesting help in many ways. These could be for fans to collect signatures or give ideas for further media coverage. Gradually fans were becoming more aware and getting involved. It was here that Craig Jessop from Hull offered to set up a web page where fans could sign online.

One morning, I was working on my computer early and decided to sort my e-mail out. What greeted me was panic. There were over one hundred e-mails with BOT on them. It was beyond my imagination what they could be. The problem was that my computer was playing up, and so I could not find out what they were.

It was mid-afternoon before it was finally discovered that it was fans signing the petition online. Craig had directed the e-mails to my computer. The signatories were from all over the UK and worldwide. Fans had signed from Malta, Australia, the Channel Islands, New York and France.

For the rest of the day, it was a major problem with a clapped-out printer, ever trying to stem the tidal wave of e-mails. As quickly as they were being printed off, more came through. Finally, at midnight, it was off to bed completely whacked. A phone call had to be made to Craig to redirect the e-mails. This was successful until finally his computer crashed. Truly, an international experience.

This now takes me onto sign online at www.rlfans.com. After losing the use of Craig's computer it was important to keep a web site open and therefore contact was made with Sadfish (Paul Cunliffe) of the Rugby League Supporters' Association. A request was made for him to set up another site, which he duly obliged with. This new site was a credit to him, as you could sign online, give comments or download petition forms. The sign online comments have come from this site and their content has been truly amazing. Thanks to Paul for all this help.

SIGN ONLINE COMMENT
(fan in Atlanta, USA)

"Bring rugby league to the USA."

Footnote

On the basis that, according to the various collectors, only about 20 out of 30,000 odd people approached had declined to sign, I make that a success rate of better than 99.9%!

3

The Petition hits the Front Page

The first time that the petition was mentioned in a newspaper was quite exciting in terms of reaching out into the local community. John Yates, a journalist on the St. Helens Reporter, had been approached about doing a feature on events. It has to be said that what happened next was not expected.

John had already done some publicity for me regarding a writing competition that was being organised by the St. Helens Writers' Circle. However, as this was media to media my thoughts were mixed. Would the petition have any impact on a local paper? No worries as John gave it the works. It made the front page of the "St. Helens Reporter" on 15.07.01, as well as being included in the Wigan version.

The above had a big bearing on matters due to many fans now believing that this fight back against media prejudice had indeed got some teeth. Was it possible that the game could bite back? When signatures were being collected round the St. Helens town centre, the effect was clear, many fans were coming over, without needing to be asked.

It was in the town centre that another amusing tale was told. An elderly couple got talking about their days of following the Saints. It appears that they had purchased a tandem and would travel from the town to places like Huddersfield and Halifax to watch their beloved team.

In those by-gone days, dad would be boss, and so they had to make excuses to sneak off. It appeared dad did not approve of the tandem and made his sweet daughter wear leggings to hide her modesty. The couple were made up because I had listened to their exploits.

Footnote

One day whilst collecting signatures in the town centre I got talking to Sarah, who frequents the Saints message board. She made me aware of someone looking over my shoulder. It just so happened to be Howard Morris, the Saints Chairman. My request for him to sign the petition was met with a dismissive smile and a condescending shake of the head and, with that, he just strolled off. It's very difficult to understand why people in positions of power can't sign a petition that is for the good of the game.

FAN'S VIEW
"Is there light at the end of the media tunnel?"

In Love with League

One refreshing aspect of the petition has been meeting the fans and realizing how they love their game with a smile. When the Saints played Castleford away, it was over to the home support to collect signatures. The fans kept me that busy it was soon kick-off time. However, the clipboard was going from one fan to another, whilst I stood there in amazement. In the end I just grabbed a load of confetti from a Cas supporter, tossed it high and cheered with them when their team came out. Being a Saint amongst the Tigers, you can imagine the hoots of laughter that greeted this!

I did in fact miss the first two Saints tries due to not being able to retrieve the clipboard. Well done Cas fans, you watch the game with a smile.

THE PETITION

Head Banger

This incredible journey certainly gave me a headache or two but none more than at the Saints versus Warrington match. At the start of the evening there was no sign of what was to come. It was a clear, crisp night as the fans drifted into the ground. As always, signatures were being collected in the Edington stand amongst the away support.

Without warning, they arrived to the sound of the bugle. Here they were following the foot soldiers. The band had arrived. Big drum, with even bigger drum major; bugler, trumpeter, yes they had arrived. Passion was etched all over their faces, some with strange hair creations and even stranger faces painted primrose and blue. It was as if they had journeyed from outer space.

It had to be admitted, though, that one and all signed the petition. However, trying to talk over the music took one mighty effort. The next day summoned me to the pill cabinet to ease my pain. Yes! They had arrived.

Paper Trail

There were other local papers that have helped cover events including: the "Liverpool Echo", "North Cumberland Times and Star", "Hull Daily Mail", "Yorkshire Evening Post", "Warrington Guardian" and "Widnes Weekly News". Apologies if any paper has been left out, but these are the only ones that are known about at the time of writing. One national paper, the "Independent", through the admirable Dave Hadfield, also gave coverage.

Not all of the above papers were receptive immediately and tenacity and salesmanship had to come to the fore. It appears that having

---

QUOTE FROM SAINTS MESSAGE BOARD
(I'm Webbo!! comments)

"Like quite a few on here, I was initially sceptical. I knew and totally agreed with the reasoning behind your need to do SOMETHING to confront the unfairness we face as a sport, but wasn't convinced a small petition from a bunch of Saints fans would achieve anything

What I didn't reason on was your (and a few others) single-minded energy and plan to get fans from other clubs to help spread it. I think it's fair to say that the momentum has taken us all by surprise.

I would say the greatest accomplishment of all has been to polarise the opinions of RL fans all over to agree something needs to be done to break the anti-RL media cycle. The petition has become a kind of rallying point. The attention it's got will ensure it can't simply be ignored.

Even if it doesn't achieve the objective of stopping the attacks on our sport in the whole of Fleet Street, it seems it has given us confidence and determination to fight to ensure our sport gets a fair deal in the face of some unwarranted and disgraceful media bullying."

---

thousands of sports fans sign a petition is sometimes not enough. Still, our thanks that they eventually gave publicity. Headlines of 'RL STRIKES BACK', 'RL CRUSADE WINS BACKING OF MP's' and 'FANS START NATIONAL MEDIA REVOLT' have all captured attention.

Listen Here

The petition gained momentum even further when it was decided to contact some radio stations. The first one to give prominence to the campaign was Wish FM, which is the local Wigan and St. Helens station. I felt the interview went well and it was subsequently broadcast the same evening and again the next day at breakfast. Another local station, Wire FM, also put out a broadcast some time later.

Such was the response that local BBC Radio could now be contacted, as we had had some good publicity and evidence of mounting signatories. BBC Radio Merseyside was the first to be contacted and an interview was done with Ian Kennedy. This was broadcast the same evening and again the following Saturday morning.

Next came BBC Radio Leeds who were very helpful with an interview and broadcast. They were particularly keen to have a follow up on the breakfast show the next day, so Sergei (Tim Hardcastle) and T-Dub (Tim Wilkinson) duly obliged. Such was the response that there was an ad hoc phone in. Tim Wilkinson, a Leeds fan, has gone on to be very helpful with the petition.

BBC Radio Humberside then made contact with me for an interview. As I was indisposed, Conboys kindly did it, and did it well. He was upset, though, as he could not have a beer at the Hull match that day!

Alan Jackson of BBC Radio Merseyside was next to do an interview and what a great presenter he is.

I had been told that mention of the petition was going to be broadcast on Radio GMR but this was never confirmed. This was some weeks before the radio interviews had been done. It was therefore decided to contact the station and enquire in my usual diplomatic way if some airtime could be given. This was to turn out a disaster.

Having made contact with a person on the sports desk I was shot down in flames. No matter how hard I tried to get my points across, the conversation was continually disrupted. The person at GMR was rude, arrogant and self-important. No matter that 20,000 fans had signed the petition, he suggested not to be so sensitive. The phone was duly put down in disgust

From the above, a letter and e-mail was duly dispatched to GMR. It was then that a phone call was received to ask if I wanted to go on air the following Thursday or Sunday. An apology was loose and only verbal. No apology has been received by post. As for the interview, it was lukewarm and done just before the news. Not too many points could be given. Listeners said that the interviewer kept interrupting. Not to worry, you can't win them all.

SIGN ONLINE COMMENT
(fan from Bordon, Hants)

"It's about time that the media in this country gave the superb athletes who play rugby league the credit they deserve."

No Return

There was one particular gripe with our very own "Rugby League Express", which is supported by the fans. Three letters had gone to Martyn Sadler at the beginning of the campaign but were never replied to. The letters were only requesting some publicity.

It was only after talking to a friend that a telephone call was made to Tim Butcher at the paper which resulted in a letter being published in the letters page. Two more letters were to be included later on. It was still felt that 20,000 signatories deserved better from 'our' paper and disappointment was felt that a feature had not been done.

At 9.40 am on the 31.08.01 it was decided to go into the lion's den, metaphorically speaking, and confront the issue. A post on the totalrl.com message board was set up mentioning the fact that letters, phone calls and faxes had not been replied to in relation to obtaining more than just letters in the letters page. The post included the fact that enormous publicity had been given by local press, radio and even Sky TV. The post finished with - "From our own TRADE PAPER there is SILENCE. The letters that have been published have had to be begged for. I don't wish to make enemies from within but I find it hard to swallow that a paper that is supposed to be on our side can ignore those fans. Sorry to be so negative, but it is 'not on' when fans are ignored from within our game."

Three message board post replies followed from Leeds Born Welsh Roots, Sadfish and John o' Gaunt, and then action. Martyn Sadler, Managing Director, left a message to say: "Of course we would be delighted to do a feature on the petition, and I have been meaning to do so for some time." It went on to apologize for various reasons and suggested contact be made with the office. Peace was restored.

Gareth Walker, a journalist on the paper, was contacted, and true to Martyn's word, an interview was given that night at the Saints versus Castleford match. A very good report was then included in the Monday edition of "League Express", for which thanks is given.

In fairness, appeals for new collectors were indeed published on the "League Express" letters page, and these did yield several volunteers.

THE PETITION

Footnote

Two requests were made to the paper to see if they wanted to include an article in the book. No feedback at all was received.

QUOTE FROM THE SAINTS MESSAGE BOARD
(Mad Saints fan)

"At first I was a bit unsure of the petition and would not help because of two things:

ONE. Who is going to take note of a petition?

TWO. What good will it do to our game if people do listen?

Both questions were wiped out as the great petition took off.

It was then realized that people would listen if many people wanted the same end result. It was never dreamed that this petition would get so many signatures and media coverage."

4

Parliament moves, but not the Chairmen

Talking of being ignored, there was another issue that needed some thought. A letter had gone to David Hinchliffe MP about the poor treatment that league receives via the media. His reply was very encouraging and included a good response. As a result of my original letter it was decided that the Parliamentary Group of Rugby League MPs would elect a Press Officer for the first time. The job of the Press Officer would be to relay to the media the work that the group undertake. Richard Caborn, the new Sports Minister, would also be invited to the group's next meeting. This was very encouraging news indeed and most welcome. (A copy of the reply is included overleaf by kind permission of David Hinchliffe MP)

Mr. Hinchliffe then suggested that it would be a good idea to let the Rugby Football League and Super League know of the initiative. Letters were accordingly sent to the RFL and Gary Hetherington in his capacity as a director of Super League (Europe). A reply was received from John Huxley of the RFL but nothing was forthcoming from Mr. Hetherington. Eventually, contact was made with Super League, but confirmation was given that no letter had been handed over.

From the above, it was decided to contact all thirty-one-league club Chairmen to see if they and their fellow directors would sign the petition. A letter, petition form and stamped addressed envelope were dispatched to all clubs. This did involve considerable work to find several of the addresses.

THE PETITION

All - Party Parliamentary Rugby League Group

HOUSE OF COMMONS
LONDON SW1A 0AA

DH/MH   25th July 2001.

Mr Ray Gent
Principal, Beacon Financial Services
Beacon House, 3 Upholland Road
Billinge, Wigan
Lancs   WN5 7JA

Dear Mr Gent,

Thank you for your letter of 26th June concerning the press coverage of Rugby League.

As you may be aware, I have personally responded to a number of the very damaging articles which have appeared concerning our sport in recent time.

Arising from your correspondence, our Group has agreed to take a number of steps.

Firstly, we have for the first time appointed a Press Officer to ensure that the work done by the Parliamentary Group receives coverage in the media and contributes to a lifting of the profile of the sport of Rugby League.

Secondly, we have agreed to invite the new Sports Minister, Richard Caborn to our next meeting with the intention of specifically pressing him on the treatment that the sport is currently receiving in the national press.

Thirdly, we are looking at a number of possible steps the Group can take in respect of directly influencing the London based press.

Obviously, we wish you well with your petition and if you feel there is any further action our Group may take, we will be happy to hear from you further.

I do feel it would be helpful if you drew the attention of the RFL and Super League to your initiative. I hope they will give you every support.

Best wishes

Yours sincerely,

David Hinchliffe MP
Secretary.

THE PETITION

As at 7.09.01, only five clubs had supported the petition. The clubs were: Hunslet, Oldham, Huddersfield, Warrington (through Lord Hoyle) and London. Maurice Lindsay, Chairman of Wigan RLFC, did have the courtesy to reply but was against the petition. There were twenty-five clubs out there who had not replied. I would ask one question: "Who is on our side?" (See later for Whitehaven and Gateshead).

SIGN ONLINE COMMENT
(fan in Bristol)

"Enough of these vitriolic and spiteful campaign propagandists pursuing their own agenda."

A True Professional

During the summer of 2001, Stew, who is the PA announcer at the Saints home matches, created a topic on the Saints message board? He was asking fans for help in how to improve his programme on match days. This included asking how other announcers sounded at away grounds. Suffice to say, fans were only too happy to oblige.

Here was a true professional at work, ever striving to go the extra mile. Stew gave prominence to the petition during several games and thanks are given here. He is a man with a refreshing attitude to the fans. Shane Richardson, the former Chief Executive of Hull Rugby League Club, also visited their message board and was known to answer fans' questions.

Others that run or administer our game at Club or Headquarters level should take note. It is not on when letters, e-mails and phone calls go unanswered. It is all well and good having a go at the media, but we do need to get our own house in order. The game sometimes lets us down with ignorance.

Well done to the Independent Supporters' Associations and Rugby League Supporters' Association for placing pressure on clubs and the game to improve matters. There is still a long way to go though, judging by events during the petition campaign. A selfish and dogmatic attitude towards the fans still prevails in our game.

QUOTE FROM SAINTS MESSAGE BOARD
(Terry Delaney comments)

"What I would like to see in any book which highlights the anomalies between media coverage of the two rugby codes, is the hypocrisy of the Rugby Football Union when they dogmatically asserted that 'Rugby is a gentleman's pastime' and imposed sanctions against any union player who associated with anyone connected with a game which was played by some teams semi-professionally.

Now that they have decided that professional rugby is acceptable after all, they expect to be given more credibility than a sport that has been professional for more than one hundred years. For any branch of the media to support them in this mis-carriage of sporting justice is an insult, and should be exposed as such."

Fight Your Own Fight

It has been interesting listening to some people's views on the game whilst collecting signatures. Several, including leading figures at club level, have asked: "What negative press?" One person was actually a prominent figure within the St. Helens club. These people either do not read the press, or do so with their eyes closed.

There are times when I have questioned what I'm doing, spending ten to fifteen hours per week on the petition. It should never be up to fans going round collecting signatures. The game should be big enough to fight its own battles. It is sad to say, though, that we are currently a disjointed sport. However, you then read another article, or listen to a radio programme that undermines the game of rugby league, and you are suddenly motivated again.

At least the game is focusing on the future with the 'Strategic Review' being designed to try and place the sport on an even keel. It is important that this works for the good of the game, else the media jackals will be chomping at the bit. More fresh meat is all they want.

Ignore the Press

I did receive a letter from Maurice Lindsay, who is the current (2001) Chairman of Wigan RLFC, in response to a request for him and his fellow directors to sign the petition. He confesses to not being a great fan of petitions and suggests that some of the problems of our game could come from within. His reply also mentions that the game is still trying to recover from a badly managed 2000 World Cup.

His advice is to ignore the press and support the game in order to return to the great standards of the 1990s. He firmly believes that the game can progress by giving its all on the field of play, as well as the game's Headquarters management adopting the same strategy and ambitions. Rather than emphasise the negative by way of a petition, let us prove them wrong by delivering the goods at Old Trafford's Grand Final and the forthcoming Test matches.

From the above, a letter was sent to Mr. Lindsay on 1.10.01 for further comment.

Dear Mr. Lindsay,

The media petition rolls on and now has over 25,000 signatories. This is a great response whether you believe in it or not.

THE PETITION

There is now a book being written on media bias and the petition from inception, right through to its conclusion. I am trying to include as many other people's views as possible. To this end, Lord Hoyle, Peter Roe and Harry Edgar have contributed, as well as many fans.

Letters have also gone out to several newspapers, the RFU and Peter Wheeler of Leicester Tigers. It is important the book is not viewed as being totally biased in favour of rugby league. If replies are received, then these will be included. If it were at all possible, would you be willing to contribute a small article?

Your letter to me stated that you were against petitions and suggested ignoring the press. Good media coverage has to be the way for any sport or business. I appreciate that the game of league has shot itself in the foot on occasions; however, some of the press articles have been very offensive and should not be part of sport. Constructive criticism is one thing, media venom another.

I look forward to hearing from you,

Yours sincerely,,
Ray Gent

SIGN ONLINE COMMENT
(fan in Reading)

"Living in the South of England, I know a lot of union supporters and they think we are not getting a fair crack of the whip."

Reply from Maurice Lindsay 04.10.01

Dear Mr. Gent,

Thank you for your second letter in respect of what you see as media bias.
You are aware of my view of the press as I explained to you in my previous

letter. Love them or loathe them you have to live with them. I have spent over twenty years in a senior capacity in rugby league ranging from Club Chairman to Chief Executive, to International Board Chairman. Everyone in sport would welcome supportive media with good coverage. Sport, however, has to earn that press support, as the media are duty bound to cover all aspects of the game including matters that are sometimes negative.

We are not blameless in generating negative opinion on occasions although I agree with you that some journalists act as 'hit and run' merchants who do not follow the sport on a regular basis. This is unfortunate but is something that we are powerless to avoid. We can only work hard to promote our game in a positive manner at all times. We do, however, seem to be a sport that has traditionally enjoyed in-fighting in spite of our own written code of conduct which tries to prevent public outbursts.

On the whole, however, I still believe that we get coverage that we deserve and probably get more space than our combined attendances actually earn in the view of some editors. Every Super League club is required to employ a full time Press Officer and this club (Wigan RLFC) will continue to try and create positive stories for the media.

Yours sincerely,
Maurice Lindsay

Whether you agree or disagree with Mr. Lindsay, I would still like to thank him for his reply.

QUOTE FROM THE SAINTS MESSAGE BOARD
(Super Saint 2001)

"I was not sure of what response you would get but, like thousands of others, I signed the petition."

THE PETITION

And One for the Sports Minister:

Dear Mr. Caborn,

It is apparent over the last year that the game of rugby league has come in for some very heavy-handed media venom. One code of rugby has been placed on top of the Christmas tree, whilst another is placed in the gutter. Our sport has always been persecuted but I can't remember so many attacks by so many newspapers.

From the above, a petition was born, of which you must now be aware. The total signatories to date are 25,000. Can so many people be wrong? This petition will be handed in to Parliament in the near future to say enough is enough. I have enclosed a sample form to show you that we are not asking for much.

During the petition campaign, I have tried to remain dignified in the face of some sewer press articles; however, the journalistic garbage enclosed (see Simon Barnes article later) *has finally been one too many. I eventually resorted to sarcasm in my reply to "The Times", as the attitude of the journalist concerned was totally unjustified. It seems to be a game of who can write the most degrading article.*

A copy has been sent to David Hinchliffe MP, who, I must say, is giving some tremendous support to our campaign for justice, as well as Lord Hoyle and other MP's. I would hope that you could reply to my letter to give further encouragement to what is a disgrace in sport.

I will finish by saying that I am ashamed to be part of this nation's sport. Freedom of press is one thing, abusing the privilege is another matter.

Yours sincerely,

Ray Gent

Following on from the above an assistant from the department of Culture, Media and Sports replied with very little encouragement in that I was referred to the Press Complaints Commission and Broadcasting Standards Commission.

He assured me that there was no favouritism for either code of rugby, or indeed any sports.

SIGN ONLINE COMMENT
(fan in Reading)

"Sick of class and prejudice from the BBC and London-based press. Give us a chance for once - our exclusion from mainstream is unfair"

5

Paper Chase - No bias here

It had been decided to send letters to four newspapers to inform them of the petition and to offer them free space in the book to see if they wished to air their views. The papers were the "Daily Mail", "Daily Express", "Mirror" and the "Sunday Times". A letter to the last-named is printed below.

Dear Sir,

There is clear evidence that certain media outlets have waged some disgraceful attacks on rugby league in recent months. From this venom, a petition was born which now has over 20,000 signatories.

A book is now being written due to the massive response the petition has had worldwide. The proposed book will look at the inception of the petition, right through to its conclusion later this year.

Media coverage of the petition has come from local press, local radio including the BBC, the independent sector and even Sky TV. This has confirmed that league fans will not continue to see their game trodden on, whilst the game of union is placed on top of the Christmas tree with all the glitter. From observing league message boards and the press, it seems that you have, or did have, a Mr. S. Jones as a journalist. It appears that he is one of the most hated men on this planet by league fans. Questions are constantly asked as to why your paper allows Mr. Jones to spout much venom against rugby league.

With the above in mind, your paper has the opportunity to feature in the book. This is being done out of fair play, as sometimes league fans are not always allowed the right of reply to adverse comment. Feel free to give your paper's views on how you see the contents of this letter.

One last point is that I think it's a poor way to treat some of your customers. Many rugby league fans are giving up buying certain newspapers due to either seeing their sport tossed into the gutter, or lack of coverage.

Yours sincerely,
Ray Gent

Alex Butler Sports Editor replies:

Dear Mr. Gent,

Many thanks for writing to the editor, who has passed your letter on to me. Unfortunately, I disagree with your main accusation that certain media outlets are "launching disgraceful attacks" on rugby league. If, by this, you mean the "Sunday Times", then I must disagree strongly.

I feel it is fair to say that we have conducted a vigorous debate about the possible merging of the two codes and that Steven Jones has been at the centre of that argument. The debate has been always lively, often bitter. But both sides have been given ample space in the paper to press their points of view.

I think it was the redoubtable Maurice Lindsay who once said: "When Steven Jones writes about union or league, people should pay attention because he knows what he is talking about."

You will excuse me if I decline to sign your petition.

Yours sincerely,
Alex Butler

Footnote

Thanks are given to Mr Alex Butler who is entitled to his opinion but the proof is in the pudding. Can thousands of fans be wrong?

THE PETITION

Alex Butler wrote another letter to say that the tide was turning as to the "Sunday Times" and its coverage of rugby league. True to his word, there have been several good articles about the game that have been professionally researched and presented. Well done the "Sunday Times" for responding and keeping its promise to improve rugby league coverage.

SIGN ONLINE COMMENT
(fan in Wimbledon)

"Why does rugby league attract such unbalanced media coverage? My conclusions are that it can only be a class thing. We are the working class upstarts that had the temerity to split from the ruling elite over one hundred years ago, and despite their best efforts, have survived since."

MEDIA WATCH / MEDIA WATCH

This book needs to highlight some of the mischief that has been going on within the media. There is no order of preference or timing. One such article found by Allan Reeve was in the "Daily Mail" of 06.08.01.

The article was referring to how great a nation Australia was in sport, even though they only had a population of only 19 million. Reference was made of how their champion sportsmen and women had dominated the world.

Over three glorious years they had been world champions at rugby union, cricket, tennis, netball, women's hockey, as well as women's and men's surfing. An apology went out to fellow Australians if one or two other sports had been missed out, as it was hard to keep up.

THE PETITION

What an insult to the game of rugby league in that Australia had become emphatic world champions only the previous year, in front of 44,000 spectators at Old Trafford and an audience of millions on Grandstand.

MEDIA WATCH / MEDIA WATCH

There was an article in very bad taste in the "Mirror" of 28.06.01. It suggested that Jason Robinson, a union convert from league, had given up twenty pints of alcohol a night to become a British Lion at union. This was a slur on his previous involvement in rugby league. To add insult to the article, there was a picture of twenty pints of beer stretched across the page.

It was well known that Jason had abstained from drink years ago to become a Christian, prompted by his friendship with Inga Tuigamala, then a rugby league player with Wigan. Jason went on to help the homeless in the Manchester area, as well as fulfilling his rugby duties.

Footnote

There was also a small article in the "Mirror" with reference to facts and figures, comparing league to union. The emphasis was to put union ahead of league. It referred to union's Cup Final of 2001 attracting 71,000 fans, whilst league's effort attracted only 58,000 fans at Old Trafford the previous autumn. Suffice to say that the paper had got the wrong game. The Rugby League Cup Final of 2001, played at Twickenham, attracted 68,000 supporters. My letter of complaint went unanswered.

QUOTE FROM SAINTS MESSAGE BOARD
(Saint Val comments)

"Well, all the media coverage on the England/Germany game got on my nerves. OK, England won, but it did not warrant half the pages of the "Mirror" the day after. Sometimes in the "Mirror" we only get one-inch by two-inch coverage for league."

MEDIA WATCH / MEDIA WATCH

Keiron Cunningham, a Saints player, caused further press mischief with his decision to turn down a lucrative deal to go and play for Swansea Rugby Union Club. This deal was to be partly funded by the Welsh Rugby Union.

After nine months of the Welsh chasing him, he confirmed his desire to stay in league. It was then suggested that he could not produce his grandfather's birth certificate to verify Welsh ancestry so he could represent Wales at union, as he had done so at league. "Stricter Union Rules" screamed the headlines.

What I can't understand is why the Welsh offered a king's ransom over a period of nine months without checking all the facts first.

On 19.08.01 the "Daily Express" ran a huge headline that suggested Keiron had been sheepish about joining Swansea due to the non-availability of the birth certificate. This half page article seemed simply a vehicle for the sulking Welsh Rugby Union to make an official statement.

THE PETITION

In any event, the said birth certificate was eventually produced and was shown on Sky TV. An apology was never forthcoming from the "Daily Express".

Footnote

The deal to keep Keiron in league was partly funded by "Club Great Britain", a new initiative by businessmen to keep players in rugby league. Even then we can't win, as the "Daily Mail" suggested the game was "desperate" when the same was applied to Kris Radlinski at Wigan. No mention of union being desperate when their game was funding the poaching of rugby league players.

MEDIA WATCH / MEDIA WATCH

There was mention of Stephen Jones from the "Sunday Times" on a previous page. Here is a man who possibly spouts more media venom against rugby league than any other journalist, or so it seems to the game's fans.

He mentions in an article on 19.08.01 entitled "Two Codes in Different Leagues" that there is nothing to gain from union merging with league, only if the union men swallowed the sport as a whole, or the possible financial collapse of league. He suggests the latter could happen but is still against the odds.

He goes on to say that rugby league's absence of commercial success, problems at the box office and lack of global appeal would mean the game has nothing to offer union. It seems strange that for a game that has nothing to offer, union has still copied many of league's innovations. Didn't union decide to turn professional? Surely union now play to a league format, including end of season play-off matches? Also copied are the yellow card, sin bin, substitutes and big screen at matches. What about union's 'poaching' of league's players and coaching staff. "Nothing to offer" seems ludicrous in the

extreme.

The article referred to Keiron Cunningham, the St. Helens hooker, and to the fact that he turned down a lucrative offer to join Swansea Rugby Union Club. It suggests that nobody in Swansea was bothered anyway. It continued that nobody had worked out yet where he could fit in, concluding that Keiron lacked the technique of a scrum half, the scrummaging power of a hooker, nor had he any experience of playing centre. Why on earth did Swansea chase him for nine months then, not to mention an awful lot of money being offered? There is also the fact of the 'missing' birth certificate that is in a previous media watch.

The criticism is offered that if union is only interested in signing the odd league player, then certainly there is nothing else to pilfer from league. Looking at the previous statements, union has pilfered much already from league. "Odd player" also seems a strange comment, when, in fact, union journalists have been suggesting every week that someone else is being targeted.

He spouts on about league being a "spectator-friendly sport without any spectators" and "The only sport that that has devoted itself to crowd pleasing, without drawing the crowds". He writes that league crowds have always struck him as being terribly tiny. Funny how current facts suggest that league does draw more crowds than union at club level, even if union crowds are rising? Even David Hinchliffe MP mentioned that union had admitted to the fact of losing 25,000 grassroots players over the last four years. Wasn't it recently published that Leeds Rhinos enjoy the biggest attendances in British club rugby of either code, with home gates bigger than second-placed Leicester Tigers?

It's interesting to note that Stephen Jones does not mention the fact that for many years, members of the armed forces were banned from playing rugby league. This was a sure way to prevent the game spreading on a wider global arena. There is also the fact that union is given the lion's share of the media hype, whilst league is trodden on.

THE PETITION

Just imagine if league had all the media attention, with union was left to the wolves? Interesting thought, this last one.

One final point is what happens if league players do switch codes? Suddenly, they seem to fit in straight away and are world-beaters. There is one headline for players staying loyal to league, whilst a different one for those who switch to union. Sheer hypocrisy.

QUOTE FROM THE HULL MESSAGE BOARD
(Shaun F)

"This petition, more than any other device, has managed to pull together the ranks of the supporters and bind them into one voice. Unseen in any other sport, it has released feelings that have lain dormant or unexpressed for various reasons. Single voices seldom rise above whispers, but the petition gives us the chance to shout at the men in charge who are content to keep our game a minority sport. It would be a great idea to contact the other countries out of the limelight, such as France, Russia, USA and PNG. Make it a worldwide thing. Who knows how big you can make it."

TELEGRAPH the News

During the petition there was grave concern for the London Broncos Rugby League Club. Virgin, who were the main sponsors, decided that they were going to draw down their involvement. Likewise, Charlton Athletic made a decision not to let the Broncos use their football stadium due to having to reseed the pitch.

If the above was not enough, then in come the tanks. The "Daily Telegraph" had a front page, full page spread in its sports section of the so-called demise. It started with the fact that Virgin, the major shareholder of the ONLY southern-based professional rugby league team, would be withdrawing their support. This bearing in mind that the company had already pumped £5 million into the ailing club.

The article moved on to what could be done, and to the fact that the club has moved from one area to another since its beginning at Craven Cottage, home of Fulham FC.

It mentioned that Super League is "desperate" to keep a toehold in the Capital, and therefore will do all it can. Comment was made to the fact that there is no logic in staying down in London as the game has survived nicely around the M62 corridor. Is this the same game that is said to be dying by media sceptics?

One other point of interest is the future headline comments if the game disappeared as a profession in London. "Rugby League sent packing back to the M62", "League can't hold its own down south", "Northern roots and northern to stay", "No one interested in League in the south." I'm sure league fans could think of a few more. The media circus would simply have a field day. And what of the dedicated fans and amateur teams that are prospering and springing up - often hosted by union clubs - throughout the length and breadth of England?

It's a sad fact that league only gets a full page spread when it's negative. The page even had a very large photo of a sparse crowd in the ground. I don't seem to recall the same response when union lost the London Scottish and Richmond clubs.

Footnote

The same paper is organizing a poll to see if soccer should use union's idea of technology at matches, for example using a big screen to re-run controversial incidents. History will show that it was league that had the big screen first. This is just another union idea, that in fact was league's. It appears that certain sections of the media cannot even begin to praise league, even if they have the right to that praise.

THE PETITION

Last Chance Saloon

Just to go the extra mile and be fair, it was decided to send letters to the papers again. This would give them one last chance to reply. Having already received correspondence from the "Sunday Times", there was still the "Daily Mail", "The Mirror" and "Daily Express".

Dear Sir,

Some weeks ago a letter was sent to you regarding the rugby league media petition. It seems that most newspapers have been jumping on the bandwagon in attacking the sport. To date 25,000 signatories have signed the petition.

Due to the worldwide response to the petition, a book is now being written. It will cover events from the inception, right through to its conclusion when it's handed into Parliament.

There is no doubt that the game has suffered from some political in-fighting and poor leadership of late, which will be included in the book. It still doesn't give the excuse for some of the journalistic trash that that rugby league has had to endure.

A request was made of your paper, out of fair play, to see if you wanted to contribute to the book. It would be appreciated if we could gather what the stance is regarding different papers' views. After all, we are supposed to be your customers, that is, those who still choose to buy a paper.

The only person to reply so far was the Sports Editor of the "Sunday Times" who couldn't find any media attacks on the sport. This was blown out of the water by Simon Barnes's article a few weeks later (copy enclosed).

I have enclosed a few other press cuttings for your perusal.

Yours sincerely,
Ray Gent

SIGN ONLINE COMMENT
(fan in Liverpool)

"I hope that this petition will get league the respect that it deserves from the media instead of the derisory and, in some cases, insulting treatment, which the sport receives at the moment."

Rugby, Rugby League, Rugby Union

The above is not to confuse the readers in suggesting there are three codes of rugby, but one could fall into the trap of thinking so, especially the unconverted.

"Free Mike McLennan" (Saints Fanzine) sums this up in these words:

"Anyone who reads the Final Hooter (fanzine) will be familiar with their crusade of pulling up media types who refer to rugby union as 'rugby'. They are excellent in picking up on the anti-league references, i.e. whenever something negative happens in union it is referred to as having happened in rugby. When something negative happens in league it is referred to as rugby league. There is no attempt to highlight the negative publicity in union."

PIG IGNORANT

POSTMAN
PIG

An example of this would be the coverage of the 'England rugby captain in drugs scandal' story. In one newspaper the text of the article referred to Lawrence Dallaglio, but unfortunately with a large picture of league's Andy Farrell on the opposite page.

David Hinchliffe MP is well known in Parliament for always referring to both codes of rugby by their full titles. This has to be the only fair way.

It is interesting regarding the current rugby union-based adverts by Zurich. These adverts completely ignore the fair approach, and only refer to rugby in a positive and biased sense. Once again they appear to be aimed at the unconverted who will think Zurich sponsors rugby rather than just rugby union. These adverts have produced some strong comment on many league messages boards. Although it does mention of union in the text, it uses the term rugby in the oral.

It may seem that the above is digressing slightly in some ways, but it does highlight how the media work in favour of one code of rugby and against another.

SIGN ONLINE COMMENT
(fan in Holyhead)

"Together we can sort out this disgusting media prejudice."

6

TV Or Not TV, That is the Question

The next stage of events was to take everyone by surprise. British Bronco from the Saints message board decided to start a thread about getting some coverage on Sky TV. At least by this time I knew what a thread was. He placed a post on the Saints message board asking for a mass e-mail campaign to get the petition mentioned on Sky TV. It must be said that many fans responded, although were not sure if Sky would take the bait.

Bets were being taken; odds were shortened, and then lengthened. Rumour had it that Ladbrokes were interested. And then it happened!

I was due to go on holiday up to the Lake District when, out of the blue, a telephone call was received A voice requested me to contact Angela Powers of Sky TV. Being early morning and switched off for the holiday, my faculties had disappeared. It was some time before it was confirmed that it was Sadfish (Paul Cunliffe of the RLSA)

On contacting Angela, it had to be explained that holidays beckoned until the following Monday, which was ten days away. After further frantic phone calls and dead ends, it was agreed that I would come back a day early for the Warrington versus Saints match. Filming then could take place before the match. It was some holiday having to telephone home to arrange the coming event.

Footnote

I had to laugh at thinking it was a wind up, as it did happen to me some years ago. June, my wife, and I had travelled down to Shropshire for the funeral of a dear friend. On the way down at Whitchurch, a delightful town in Shropshire, disaster struck. June's eye suddenly started to bleed and we had to divert to a nearby hospital for treatment. Suffice to say, we missed the funeral and could only apologize to our dear friend's son.

On getting home I felt completely whacked and was ready for a cup of tea. It was then that I received a phone message asking me to contact a number. On ringing up there was an angry voice asking why I had not been in as arranged. Trying to explain was impossible, as the voice continued to interrupt. Not feeling in the best of sorts I suddenly let out with: "I've just travelled 200 miles to a funeral, had problems on the way and now you **!*!! come on here demanding answers to a non-event!" That was what I thought until Brian, my niece's husband, rang up. Yours truly had been had. It was a Mr. Angry pre-recorded phone message.

Anyway, back to Sky TV. Filming was duly completed, with a follow up interview on the Tuesday. All in all it was a brilliant coup for British Bronco and fans on the Saints message board. (Do I get a free season ticket for all the Saints plugs?) Many thanks to BB, my cousin Agent Mulder (good line in banners), John o' Gaunt and family and Allan Reeve for helping with events. Special, special thanks to my wife June for putting up with me.

Sky did us proud, especially Angela Powers, the cameraman, Stevo and Edie Hemmings. When the piece was broadcast Stevo was ready to take his hammer down to London to hit a few heads. The remark caused hoots of laughter, but really did put the icing on the cake. Special thanks also to the doormen at Warrington Rugby League Club. Big lads though they were, they were very helpful and friendly.

Allan Reeve has also encountered nothing but friendliness at

Warrington. When he and his family went there to collect signatures at a game, Lord Hoyle let the two children in for nothing, as did Salford on a similar exercise.

The result of this media coverage was that it made collecting signatures easier. Suddenly fans were taking the petition clipboard to be signed without the need to be asked. It also cemented fans' views that at last this petition could have some clout.

The total was rising.

Contact was made with Granada and Yorkshire TV, but sadly there was no response.

SIGN ONLINE COMMENT
(Fan from Herts)

"I had stopped buying papers and had given up hope of a fair deal, that is until the petition was mentioned on Sky TV"

THE PETITION

Auntie Beeb!

Mainstream BBC has also got some questions to answer in the course of time. It is common opinion amongst rugby league fans that the BBC thinks they are doing our game a big favour, whilst the fans think the opposite!

In 2001, BBC Radio 5 Live had a phone-in topic about rugby league dying. According to the presenter, Nicky Campbell, this controversial broadcast had more e-mail and phone responses than any previous programmes. It was suggested that the presenter was taken aback by people's responses. Even BBC Newsnight had a go saying the game was dying and had no support. I suspect it is safe to say that none of the presenters involved have ever experienced a live game.

Mention was made earlier in the book about the BBC's sarcastic comments about the 2000 RL World Cup opening match. Neutrals may say rugby league fans are paranoid, yet we do not make such accusations up without firm evidence. So much simply drops into our lap.

The Super League show that goes out on BBC 2 on a Sunday is a summary of the weekend's league games, preview and topical discussion. Even then, given the paucity of the BBC's portfolio of sport, it is only shown 'up north'. Many fans south of Lancashire and Yorkshire and north of the border ask why they cannot receive the programme. The same old response is: "Nobody is interested in other parts of the country." An e-mail was sent to the BBC about the above situation, but without any reply.

The Super League Show that featured the 2001 Grand Final, the climax to the season in front of a record 60,000 fans at Old Trafford (the biggest sporting event in England that weekend) was deemed by the BBC's programme planners to be of less interest to the BBC's national audience than a repeat episode of 'Cagney and Lacey'.

I would be interested to learn the viewing figures for that particular TV 'classic'. Of course, no e-mail response was forthcoming from Peter Salmon at the BBC.

E-mailing Peter Salmon is a favourite pastime of many fans. His excuses for not showing the Super League Show nationally vary each time, with no consistent answer.

QUOTE FROM THE SAINTS MESSAGE BOARD
(Roger Moore@Wire)

"Having stood at Super League Clubs, as well as academy and amateur games, I'd like to endorse the way the petition is bringing fans together. Only a rare few refuse to sign, with the rest only too willing."

Bath Time with the Beeb

Matt Anniss lives in Bath in the West Country. His views on the Beeb make fascinating reading:

For rugby league fans outside the heartlands of Northern England, following the 'Greatest Game' can be a frustrating experience. Those of us who haven't got the cash to shell out for satellite TV have to make do with meagre reports in national newspapers, occasional reports on Radio Five Live and the BBC's on-off relationship with our beloved sport.

While the rantings of Stephen Jones ("The Times") and Frank Keating ("The Guardian") get our goat, it's the attitude of the Beeb that drives others nuts. For those of us who care about rugby league, the almost total lack of decent coverage by Britain's public service broadcaster makes our blood boil. Each week brings new grievances: Nicky Campbell sneering down his nose at the Northern Ford Premiership; Radio Five ignoring the Ashes decider the morning after the Test; Rob Bonnet predicting the demise of the game every other Monday on breakfast. The list goes on.

Each snotty remark raises our ire another notch, and prompts a barrage of e-mails to head of sport, Peter Salmon, from irritated Leaguies. "Sort it out!" we scream. In response, nothing.

On paper, many of the things that drive us nuts are minor. We would argue that they make up a small part of a much larger catalogue of Auntie annoyances, but that's not the point. For rugby league to thrive, survive and, we hope, reach a new audience, widespread terrestrial TV and national radio coverage are essential. Widespread promotion of televised Challenge Cup games or Monday morning reports on the weekend's Super League games would do wonders, as would decent marketing and promotion from the game's governing body (but, hey, we can't have everything).

The relationship between the BBC and rugby league has always been a strange one. Ever since they first began televising Challenge Cup Finals in the 50s, the bosses at Television Centre have grudgingly recognised the existence of rugby's forbidden code. The early years saw the sport portrayed as a quirky Northern Cult enjoyed by men who wore flat caps and bred whippets in brick outhouses.

Throughout the 60s and 70s, television viewers grew to associate rugby league with the homely Yorkshire tones and quaint Northern catchphrases of Eddie Waring. While there's no doubting Waring's immense passion and love for the sport, his continued presence behind the microphone did little to discourage the stereotype of a sport confined to the working class areas of the North.

In my day job, I regularly speak to non-rugby league fans down in the West Country. Those that don't follow union (which is most people, even in this hotbed of union) have little knowledge of league. If pressed, they often mention Eddie Waring, his successor Ray French, or something about flat caps and whippets. Fast-forward thirty years and little has changed.

While Sky have tried hard to portray the sport as a game played by athletic supermen, the BBC seem stubbornly attached to outdated stereotypes they consciously helped to create. They seem to believe that people outside the M62 corridor have little interest in league, despite mounting evidence to the contrary. The fact that TV ratings for live Challenge Cup games on Grandstand are repeatedly higher than rugby union's Heineken Cup, one of the BBC's most high profile assets, just reinforces the perception in league circles that dear old Auntie is a bastion of anti-league bias.

It may seem far-fetched to some, but leaguers have been paranoid about such matters for years. When I was at school, I once did an English Language assignment where I interviewed various rugby league people about the development of the game in Sheffield and South Yorkshire. The biggest interview was with the then Sheffield development officer, Ralph Rimmer, now Chief Executive of Huddersfield Giants. When we got on to the media and rugby league, Ralph had one thing to say: beware of the Oxbridge mafia. "The BBC," he told me, "is full of ex-public schoolboys, the old school tie brigade who look down on rugby league as the product of greedy working class Northerners."

At the time, I took what he said on board, as it seemed to make sense: why else would the Beeb's coverage be so bad? As time went on, I forgot about Ralph's words of wisdom I had other things to worry about. Then something happened that changed my perception of the BBC for good.

I was in my third year of a Multi-Media Journalism degree at Bournemouth University when Charles Runcie, the corporation's Head of Sports Newsgathering, came down to give us a guest lecture. From the start, Runcie fitted my exact stereotype of BBC bosses. He was a Scottish, ex-public schoolboy who played and enjoyed union. Every sentence he spoke dripped with arrogance. Within minutes of the lecture beginning, I was already seething with rage.

Contrasting the BBC's sports coverage with that of Sky Sports, he singled out the satellite channel's Super League coverage as something he particularly hated: "It's all hype, and people don't like hype." But that was nothing compared to his next bombshell, claiming that league was nothing but "Big blokes bashing into each other."

Everyone in my seminar group turned and looked at me: I was shaking my head in disbelief. Such was my rage that I cornered Runcie after the lecture and asked him if he really believed what he said; I can't remember his exact words, but it did little to change my mind.

Subsequently, Runcie's outburst made it to the news pages of "Total Rugby League" magazine. The guys at League Publications, for whom I'd written articles on and off for a few years, were ecstatic: they always thought the Beeb was biased and now they had some ammo to prove it.

Of course, Charles Runcie wasn't best pleased, got heavy with my course leaders and I was threatened with disciplinary action for bringing the course into disrepute. League Publications and various rugby league journalists rallied round, ringing my course leaders and generally kicking up a fuss. In the end, the saga made the pages of "Private Eye", something of which I'm immensely proud. (I still have the cutting hanging on my wall).

Charles Runcie is just one example of what rugby league is up against at the BBC. Many of their top radio presenters, John Inverdale, Nicky Campbell and numerous sports reporters, take every opportunity to do league down, while head of sport, Peter Salmon, doesn't seem to give two hoots about Britain's second-biggest spectator sport. Contrast league's paltry coverage of a few Challenge Cup games and occasional commentaries on Radio Five with the hours and hours of airtime dedicated to rugby union games.

As a national broadcaster, they have a remit to cover a wide range of sports; it's in their Royal charter. This they do, giving hours and hours of coverage to rowing, athletics and other marginalized sports. They think, for some reason, that union, with its higher profile, is a game enjoyed by a large proportion of the viewing public. Strangely, most of the people I speak, to largely non-league followers, tell me exactly the opposite: they think union is boring.

Still, why let the opinions of viewers get in the way of the pursuit of your own interests? Whether the BBC really is a bastion of anti-league bias is debatable for such sweeping statements are hard to prove without months of intricate research, but the corporation certainly does our sport few favours. One thing is certain: without the support of the BBC, rugby league has no way of reaching the majority of the British population. Some would say rugby league needs the BBC more than the Beeb needs rugby league. Sadly, they don't think they need us at all.

Matt Anniss is the Music Editor of International DJ magazine and a former contributor to "Rugby League Express" and "Total Rugby League". He lives in Bath, where he spends most weekends arguing with rugby union supporters about the merits of the thirteen-a-side code. He is currently writing a book about the recent history of Sheffield Eagles, to be published in the summer of 2002

SIGN ONLINE COMMENT
(fan in Leigh)

"The recent coverage by the media of the long running feud between the Rugby Football League and Rugby Union has been rather biased towards the RFU. How can we as a sporting nation expect to reach the pinnacle of any sport when media writes so unfairly of one sport and praises another? When will we learn that having a free press does not mean that they have a right to distort the facts and views of the public at large?"

7

T-Dub goes Clubbing...

Tim Wilkinson was given a mention earlier in the book and has been kind enough to give his thoughts on events. Even though some matters have been mentioned earlier, it is still nice to reiterate and bring good points to the fore.

The Greatest Game - of Indifference

"The players never let us down". Rugby league fans say it; Eddie Hemmings of Sky TV can't stop saying it. True enough, but how do the club administrators measure up in terms of supporting the profile of the game in general?

Surely, the people with the greatest financial interest in the game (those in the clubs' boardrooms) and those with the greatest physical commitment to the game (the coaches and players) would want fair representation in the papers and on television for their endeavours?

Funnily enough, it seems not!

As well as capturing a sample of the volume of public feeling about media neglect, expressions of support from a few senior figures within the game would add a bit of gravity to the campaign, so let's see what they came up with.

FAN'S VIEW

"There are some good men in our game, and then there are those with self-interest!"

THE PETITION

Petition Support (or otherwise) - Boardroom

In the petition's early days, Ray Gent wrote to the Chairmen/Chief Executives of all 31 clubs asking for their co-operation and support for the campaign. A brief reply would have been nice; maybe even on club headed notepaper. Maybe just a phone call, even if only to what it was all about. A surprisingly thin response was received.

Lord Hoyle signed for Warrington with a short letter of support. Just the sort of response needed to give further encouragement.

Other than Warrington, only Directors of Oldham, Hunslet, Huddersfield and London replied positively by signing a petition sheet. Thanks, but what of the others?

Whitehaven subsequently added their support via the good offices of RL stalwart Harry Edgar, who in the meantime had just got involved with the club's administration.

Gateshead was another club that also added their support via Mark Wightman who sent in 74 petition signatures. Not only is Mark a director, but also mans the stall before match days as well as compiling stats.

A senior employee of Bradford was happy to sign the petition on a personal basis outside the Racecourse ground at Wrexham before the Wales v England international, but no official response from anyone else at the "People's Team'.

Nothing, either, from the 'biggest rugby league club in the northern hemisphere', Leeds, who seem wary of anything that might be viewed as prejudicial to their rugby union aspirations.

More negatively, Maurice Lindsay declined to support the petition at all with the advice that those concerned should 'ignore the press'. Strange for one who could be said to court it so frequently? Still, at least he took the trouble to reply.

So much for the 'suits'...

> ### SIGN ONLINE COMMENT
> (Fan from Richmond, Surrey)
>
> *"Hmmmmmm! Don't I live and play in the South? I find it particular irritating that both the BBC and newspaper editors allow the views of rugby union loving journalists to be presented to the country without any balance in the form of a right to reply from any credible rugby league person."*

Petition Support - Coaches and Players
Is There Anybody Out There?

Taking a break from gathering petition signatures from mere mortals, I took it upon myself to look for signs of life elsewhere within our clubs.

It must be desperately disappointing for a coach or player to open a newspaper and find nothing but football speculation, racing results and everything but a decent report of the cracking match he was involved with the night before. Would those whose livelihood is the game on the field be prepared to get involved with the campaign for a fairer crack of the whip at recognition of their efforts?

Again, a limited response.

On the subject of solidarity within the game, the club leading from the front has certainly been Hull. The then Chief Executive Shane Richardson's forthright backing for the game against its detractors has been second to none, with similar commitment from Coach Shaun McRae. Even as 'incomers' to Britain, would lie down and die for rugby league.

Here are two people who know what the game means to the

game's supporters, in terms of pride and responsibility to those who were at their club before them and those in the future. They feel it too and aren't afraid to voice it. Shaun and the Hull players were early signatories to the petition.

Warrington players gave early support too.

Signatures collected on a clipboard left at the Castleford office yielded the senior figures of Allan Agar, Colin Maskill and Dean Sampson, on an individual basis, but nothing on behalf of the club's coach.

Later, further Cas players signed at a club shop open day, and huge thanks to the staff at both Cas souvenir shops for hosting a clipboard each. Cas Panthers amateur RLFC too.

Meanwhile Ray informs me that Wigan and Saints players signed the petition, as well as Ian Millward the Saints coach and Billy Boston the Wigan legend.

Seeking some sort of commitment from the coaches, I circulated the remaining nine Super League club Coaches and 13 of the Northern Ford Premiership clubs on 22.08.01 with the following letter:

Dear Sir,

I would guess that as a lover of the Greatest Game, you and your players are heartily sick of the national media's constant denigration of rugby league, as are many of the rest of the RL fraternity. It seems impossible for some to write about RL without a negative spin.

Over recent years this has degenerated from mockery of the 'cloth cap and brass band' image of the game to the sheer malevolence we have to read so regularly. It must be particular disheartening for those striving to establish the game in non-traditional areas, such as the Summer Conference clubs, Armed forces, Scotland, Ireland and Wales etc. to read regular reports predicting the game's death.

A 'fair treatment by the media' petition has been running for about four months now and has featured in such publications as the "Yorkshire Evening Post" and "League Express", with coverage on Radio Leeds, Wire FM, Wish FM, Radio Merseyside, and Humberside etc.

After years of individual efforts, the internet has enabled this to be a co-ordinated initiative, across the whole of the country. Collectors are working in many rugby league towns and cities, as well as other places scattered far and wide.

Whilst this is purely a fans' initiative, the Rugby League Supporters' Association website (rlfans.com) is helping by hosting the principal copy and acting as a meeting point for those who have stood up and got involved.

The current number of signatories is fast approaching 20,000 (now that's impressive, you've got to say), and aims for a total in excess of 25,000 by the last GB versus Australia Test, after which it will be delivered to Parliament.

Signatories also include the St. Helens, Warrington, Wigan and Hull teams, plus a host of other players. Ray Gent, who started the whole thing off and acts as coordinator, has received a letter of support from David Hinchliffe.

I attach a copy of the petition and wonder if you and your players, on a personal basis, would be willing to sign. This would be a tremendous boost and add further credibility to the effort.

Many thanks and I hope to hear from you.

Yours sincerely
Tim Wilkinson

Some of the coach's positions were uncertain, with the usual managerial merry-go-round. Also, for example, the Keighley club, were in receivership at the time. Some other clubs were between coaches. Attempting to fill the gaps in my NFP knowledge by using the internet, I couldn't readily locate details of the remaining six clubs. (If I couldn't readily find them on the internet after trying hard, how would a potential sponsor get on? But that's another subject.)

Letters were sent to the bashful nine Super League clubs who hadn't responded to Ray's boardroom approach, and the 13 Northern Ford clubs whose whereabouts weren't ex-directory, in hopeful expectation. The postman doesn't always call on St. Valentine's Day. Either way, the next week or two felt like a mild case of being stood up.

Where was everyone?

It may be the case that some of the NFP coaches were on holiday out of season, or, being part time, otherwise occupied in gainful employment away from the game. But in that case surely someone keeps an eye on his or her post.

Alternatively, it may be the case that none of the remaining SL coaches could be bothered to reply, had their post vetted or intercepted, or had been warned off by others in authority at their clubs. I suspect a bit of both, but it still can't explain why. How is registering a vote of support for a campaign for fairness in any way contentious?

At least one of the missing SL coach's had time for us. John Harbin, then at Wakefield Trinity, was consistently forthright in his defence of perceived 'everyone's out to get us' treatment he felt that his club had been subjected to during the 2001 season. It was no surprise then that his name and those of many of his players found there way onto a petition sheet, which was quickly returned.

The other honourable exception was Peter Roe, then the coach of Featherstone Rovers and Assistant Coach of Yorkshire, now at Wakefield Trinity. Peter was only too keen to comment and, after ringing me at home, he took the trouble to send a stinging commentary on the game by e-mail, and then phone me to check it had arrived

Peter Roe, Head Coach of Featherstone Rovers Rugby League Club (now Head Coach of Wakefield Trinity) comments:

"I fully endorse the rugby league petition with regard to the amount of negative publicity frequently 'spun' like the proverbial spider's web by our so called journo's whose southern bias toward, in particular the 15 man code, is an obvious attempt to squeeze out anything positive which takes place in the 'greatest

game'

The usual pre-prepared statement the national papers issue is that the 13-man game is northern based so for that reason they cannot sell newspapers. We all know, without sounding paranoid, that there is a deeper hidden agenda to which the nationals work.

There is an inherent hate for the game of rugby league based on the historic working class uprisings such as Luddism, Mercantilism, and broken time payments. It reminds them of revolution, working rights and left wing politics.

Rugby league, to many anti rugby league people, bears an inherent stigma passed down through the ages.

The worm has now turned, for the thing we were most hated for was payment for playing. Rugby league players were not only banned from simply playing union but also from union clubhouses, a social stigma with which a player became categorised. Sporting apartheid became prevalent. Now rugby union are doing what for years they hated us for. We don't ban a league player if he goes to union, we wish him well.

The rugby union press still have a problem as they still refuse to recognise rugby league. On many occasions, they breach the Human Rights Act when they denigrate our game. I can easily name them but live in fear of the midnight knock on the door - am I liable for action?

I fully back anything which will lead to the rules of fair play being laid down to flush out into oblivion the anti rugby league apartheid press."

The above is Peter's own opinion and not necessarily the opinion of those connected to Featherstone Rugby League Club, nor his new club of Wakefield Trinity. If only others had similar fire in their belly...

Polite follow-up letters were sent to the 'missing' Super League coaches and the 12 non-responding NFP clubs plus the remaining 6 NFP clubs I'd subsequently tracked down. This went on the 9.10.01:

THE PETITION

Dear Sir,

I attach a copy of a letter sent to you on 22.08.01, regarding the petition for fairer coverage of rugby league in the national media, which you might have seen on SKY sports and in the local papers and "League Express". Having only scratched the surface of the potential, some 25,000 signatures have already been collected, with more to come. The general public has backed this voluntary initiative with the majority keen to sign. These will be submitted to Parliament via David Hinchliffe MP when the petition closes after the GB versus Australia Tests.

It would therefore be a great help if a few more senior figures within the game, in terms of coaches and players, showed some sort of support.

From the original letter circulated, the response was desperately poor. It would be terrible to think that only a few of the current SL and NFP coaches asked could be bothered to register their support for a campaign that seeks to improve the disappointing coverage the game receives from the national media, something that surely we all want.

A brief note, on club paper, or a signature on a petition form would be gratefully received. Again, this is a voluntary initiative done by a small group of fans at our own expense and in our own time. It would be great to hear that as well as ordinary fans; the campaign also has the backing of those who do have a voice within the game.

Yours sincerely,
Tim Wilkinson

SIGN ONLINE COMMENT
(Fan in London)

"The mere fact that we have to do this is sickening."

THE PETITION

The two further responses have been Sheffield's talisman Mark Aston and his players and Mike Ford and the Oldham team. Otherwise the deafening sound of silence prevailed.

Club Loyalty to the Code?

The Rugby League Supporters' Association undertook a similar 'show your true colours' exercise at the time of the notorious Peter Wheeler comments. A hornet's nest had been stirred up by Mr. Wheeler's speech at a 2001 RU British Lions post tour dinner where he commented that the Twickenham hierarchy had been in discussion with the rugby league clubs about the possibility of their switching codes to play union.

This may have been partially true, an exaggeration or merely gin-fuelled hyperbole, but such was the wholesale reporting of this as sacrosanct fact that an already sensitive RL public, fed on an almost daily diet of Harris/Henry Paul/Cunningham defection speculation, was moved to lynch-mob pitch.

What to do? Sparked by Mr. Whelan, Shane Richardson, then Chief Executive at Hull, incandescent at his Super League colleague's threat to take the Wigan club to union, called for clubs to sign a 'loyalty pledge' to their future within the game.

Possibly a 'loose cannon' comment, but with the tide of media speculation again building up against the game, the RLSA seized on Mr. Richardson's idea and took matters into their own hands. On the 19.7.01 the RLSA faxed each of the 31 SL and NFP clubs with a request for a commitment of loyalty to the league code. These were to be returned by fax.

Some 14 clubs responded. (Twelve positives were Hull Leigh, Oldham, Salford, London, Warrington, Bradford, Castleford, Halifax, Gateshead, and Huddersfield). Leeds replied, generally positively but somewhat ambiguous.

The 17 others either didn't reply at all, or apparently can't operate a fax machine.

The main dissenter was Wigan. Consistently, Wigan rejected the request and in declining to respond on the subject famously 'refused to be distracted' from the season long process of winning the Super League crown.

At least the exercise brought Mr. Whelan's thoughts to the fore by admitting to having such discussions with persons unknown within rugby union. This may have been a bluff in Mr. Whelan's campaign against the Salary Cap that he felt was hindering his club's ability to compete for the most expensive players, as well as retain others within league already. There again he could have meant it.

More on Wigan's reluctance from Ray, later...

Either way, the threat of wholesale club defections could only undermine the already unstable image of the game and its future, discourage future potential sponsors and disenfranchise supporters.

Whatever the validity of the exercise and the legal worth of the faxes returned, given the opportunity to nail their colours to the rugby league mast at a time when the game itself was under attack, a surprising number of clubs didn't bother.

Actions speak louder than words, and 17 out of 31 senior clubs couldn't manage either.

Footnote

The salary cap is a contentious issue and will not be debated here. Suffice to say; depending on which club is involved, there are reasons for and against. It was brought in to try and control clubs' finances. On the one hand, there are those that say it restricts clubs from buying the best players, as well as retaining other top stars in the game. On the other, there are those that say it puts pressure on the other clubs to compete and therefore encourages excessive spending. That's as much as I am saying.

A request was also made of Mr. Whelan to see if he would sign the petition. "What negative press?" came the reply.

SIGN ONLINE COMMENT
(Fan in Wigan)

"As a young player I applaud this radical move to ensure the future of our great sport."

So Thanks for the Effort, Lads...

Let's not get carried away, the media petition isn't going to change the world, but it has a role to play and is serving a purpose.

In terms of starting to quantify the depth and strength of public feeling that many throughout the game suspected existed, the petition has established that feeling amongst everyday leaguies runs deep, strong and bitter in ample quantities.

Most of the nation doesn't have the balance of unprejudiced journalism that exists in rugby league's so called 'northern strongholds'. If "The Guardian" says, "Great game, RL, shame it has to die," (F Keating), after a while it becomes perceived wisdom.

Whose job is it to challenge that? How does a coach trying to recruit players in a development area fight against that kind of tide?

Having been backed by the public, equally the campaign deserves some sort of recognition from those in the limelight of the game that it seeks to assist.

Maybe our esteemed blazers don't have an opinion on anything that happens outside of their clubs' gates. Maybe they are oblivious to public perception of the game as it sinks below the horizon of public view, the way boxing has similarly slipped out of the media's sight since turning to satellite.

Is it possible in their own small town worlds that it doesn't matter that the image portrayed to potential sponsors and investors is of a marginalized, parochial game, on the back foot and too battle weary to complain about those who go out of their way to paint it so?

In contrast to the hoards of fans that have flocked to sign, it's a shame that of the 'household names' who run our clubs and have a voice, most have been reluctant to spare five minutes to use it.

Six expressions of support out of 31 clubs from the boardroom.

Nine responses out of 31 clubs from the training ground.

Thirteen positive responses out of 31 clubs willing heed a call from a SL club Chief Executive and sign a pledge of commitment to the league code.

Not a brilliant reflection, especially on those clubs who failed to respond to any of the three approaches.

Still, at least the players never let us down...

SIGN ONLINE COMMENT
(Fan in Dublin)

"Enough is Enough"

8

Part of the Union

There was an interesting conversation with a friend at this time. It had been mentioned that rugby league players were banned for many years from playing union, all as a result of players being paid. His argument was why should it be okay for union players to be paid now, yet not in the past?

He went on to suggest that many top union players had been offered nice easy jobs so that they could pursue their "amateur" game. Others were paid so called "boot money". This does not add up, as it is rugby league that is being targeted by many rugby union writers.

From the above, it was decided to write to the English RFU at Twickenham on 11.09.01 to see if there might be an apology for the injustice of the past (some hope) and to gauge their views on the book. The letter is printed below.

Dear Sir,

"And now for a game that no one cares about, Rugby League." This was an article heading in a national newspaper late last year. It was an appalling attack on a sport and was full of sarcasm.

Since the above, there has been more media venom that is trying to downgrade rugby league to the gutter, whilst placing rugby union at the top of the Christmas tree with all the glitter.

Now I have nothing against those that wish to play union but do find events a disgrace. One newspaper was even calling league hypocrites. The real hypocrites surely were the men in charge of union over the years.

Professional rugby league players and some amateurs were banned from playing rugby union, yet it is now acceptable to pay union players today. It was common knowledge that top union players received 'boot money', whilst others were given nice easy jobs, so that they could remain AMATEUR. I was also banned from playing rugby league whilst a member of the armed forces.

Will there ever be an apology from the RFU over the injustice that the above created?

There is now a media petition circulating that has gone worldwide and has currently over 20,000 signatories. League fans are now saying enough is enough? They don't mind constructive criticism but deplore this media bias and attack.

From the petition a book is being written outlining its inception, right through to its conclusion later this year. Out of fair play, the RFU has the opportunity to contribute to the book. Please feel free to air your views on the contents of this letter, which will be included in the book.

Yours sincerely,
Ray Gent

SIGN ONLINE COMMENT
(Fan in Burnham on Sea)

"I refuse to buy the papers that snub rugby league and always will."

My offer of a sporting olive branch fell on deaf ears, as there was no reply.

THE PETITION

Another Petition

A letter was sent to Mr. Wheeler, Chief Executive of Leicester Tigers. Enclosed with the letter was a request for the Leicester players to sign the petition to support one sport for another. The letter was much the same as the ones that were sent to the press and the Rugby Football Union. It outlined events that have gone on within the media against rugby league, as well as requesting comment for the proposed book. Mr. Wheeler has kindly replied and confirmed by phone that the letter can be published. This is bearing in mind that the views are those of Mr. Wheeler, and not necessarily those of anyone else connected with Leicester Tigers RUFC.

Dear Mr. Gent,

Thank you for your recent letter regarding the petition you are organising on behalf of rugby league fans.

I must admit I am not aware of the media bias against rugby league that you suggest in your letter, and certainly nothing that I have read in newspapers would give me that view. It may be that I am reading the wrong newspapers or that the articles you refer to only appear regionally. Certainly sitting where I am I am infuriated by what I perceive to be **BIAS TOWARDS RUGBY LEAGUE**, *especially by the BBC and certainly by Radio 5.*

Everybody that I know in professional rugby union has the utmost respect for professional rugby league, the game, the clubs and the players, and we ought not to allow the press or any other outside agency to stir us into fighting each other when there may be great benefit with us talking constructively with each other.

I am not sure from the wording of your petition whose views it is aimed at changing because the press will write what they want to irrespective of petition.

Yours sincerely,
Peter Wheeler

THE PETITION

First of all I would like to thank Mr. Wheeler for his reply. As you can see from the letter, there are four words highlighted. The letter had to be read several times to make sure it wasn't a dream. The words **'BIAS TOWARDS RUGBY LEAGUE'** will have many league fans scratching their heads. A phone call had to be made to Mr. Wheeler to make sure it wasn't a misprint.

Now this comment certainly gives food for thought!

Mr. Wheeler confirmed that the letter wording was correct. He also confirmed that he had only recently written to Radio 5 to complain about of lack of union coverage. I will have to leave this to the readers, as it certainly puts the cat amongst the pigeons.

SIGN ONLINE COMMENT
(Union Fan in Loughborough)

"Being a union fan I fully agree with your petition but I still say union is the better game"

Footnote

I suppose a petition will have to be started for rugby union. Could turn out to be a profitable business. Petitions U.K. sounds okay to me. Canvassers and secretary required.

9

A Grand Day Out

It's now Grand Final week, with the Bradford Bulls due to meet the Wigan Warriors in the Old Trafford decider. There is still some time to go as regards the petition, and no doubt fans will be collecting signatures at the forthcoming match.

Looking back over events, it somehow seems a dream. It was never envisaged at the beginning that 25,000 signatures would be obtained. The fact that the petition has spread worldwide and reached its peak on television seems something out of a fantasy. There was also the press coverage and local radio interviews. Now that matters have calmed down, I have to pinch myself that it did happen. The pace of it all just took me along, like some white-knuckle ride at the fairground.

There are still other contributions to come in regarding the book, although some of the press and The Rugby Football Union have yet to reply, if at all they will.

What now of the petition? David Hinchliffe MP has been in touch and suggested we hand the petition over during quieter moments. This will be done down in London with as much publicity as possible. It's important to have plenty of media coverage to give it some clout.

The most common question during the summer has been: "Will it do any good?" This is very difficult to ascertain at this time, although one would hope for some response. I feel the petition has to serve as a springboard to be used in the coming months and years.

THE PETITION

Pressure, pressure, pressure has to be maintained if we are ever going to get some respect and decent coverage.

With regards to pressure, there is now a fans' media group being set up. The aim is to help the game of rugby league overcome media bias and promote it to various media outlets. With this in mind, at least the petition is there for any group to use as a starting point. There is still a long way to go before league can finally free itself from the mantraps.

The game has to get its act together in terms of moving forward with confidence. Evidence in the book suggests that as a sport we have been shortsighted at times. The in-house fighting, politics and selfish attitudes have only served to hold the game back.

For anyone suggesting that we ignore the press, then I have this comment to make. I was reading a message from Jules of Luton on the Saints message board. Jules had been a convert to rugby league this year and spent much of her time travelling up to watch the Saints. In her own words: "My mates at work thought I was foolish to support a dying game."

The last sentence above needs repeating: "My mates at work thought I was foolish to support a dying game." The point about the game dying has been mentioned in the press, Radio 5 and BBC 2 this year, as well as from Frank Keating of The Guardian amongst others. The media is a powerful weapon for good or bad. Media definitely influences many people and all attempts should be made to win it over.

It was interesting when I met a broker representative from Scottish Widows at a seminar. On coming over to talk, it was mentioned that he thought he knew me. After deliberating he said: "You are the person that was on Sky TV. I signed your petition at Bradford." If one is told that a sport is dying, then eventually it will stick in people's minds, just like the chap from Scottish Widows remembering me.

After the Grand Final there are three Test matches against the

Aussies, as well as four club games versus the old foe. Obviously this depends on the current war on terrorism. There is talk that the Aussies may not come over for fear of safety. Only time will tell if the events are to take place. If the Test matches do go ahead, then it will be interesting to see what the media make of it all.

SIGN ONLINE COMMENT
(Fan in Warrington)

"Come on you league fans, let's hear your voices, support the sport."

It's Not All Over Yet!

Sad to say, we seem to be back to square one. The article that started the petition ball rolling appeared just after the Challenge Cup final. Now, after the Super League Grand Final, Simon Barnes for "The Times" has written another derogatory article. I have tried to remain dignified during the petition campaign but this new attack is one too many.

The piece concerned is titled: "Final that signalled beginning of the end". Apparently, students in the year 2050 are asked to study a video of the 2001 Super League Grand Final and come to a conclusion as to why the game died and the two rugby codes eventually merged, presumably under union rules. Nothing less would do for the very eloquent Mr. Barnes. The piece refers to the commentator on the said match, Eddie Hemmings, and to the fact that he is describing the game so: "the fixture is etched on the sporting psyche of the nation" and "the eyes of the sporting world are turned to Old Trafford".

This article did extol the virtues of fit, professional rugby league players, who were said to be highly accomplished in handling and speed compared to players like Gareth Chilcott, the ex-England international, who were unfit. Furthermore, it went on to say that in the past, rugby union players, as amateurs, couldn't match their league counterparts. Can't remember these accusations being targeted against union in times gone by.

Now that the game of rugby union has decided to come clean (see previous misdemeanours) and pay players 'legally' it is a different ball game. It continues on the basis that union now has the 'sexy' annual Six Nations Championship (international matches played every year between England, Scotland, Ireland, Wales, France and Italy), something league, as a club-based game, cannot aspire to.

Some mention was made of the fact that union was now attracting the floating voters of television sports and therefore the flow of money was all one way. Downgrading league and upgrading union is a great way to sway those floating voters.

He finishes the article with the supposedly humorous epithet: "Essay: The 2001 Grand Final made the merging of the two codes inevitable. Discuss."

Footnote

A guy called Craig mentioned on one of the internet message boards that Simon Barnes was from Wigan and was a good reporter. You wouldn't find Dave Hadfield of the "Independent" writing such a piece about rugby union.

SIGN ONLINE COMMENT
(Fan in Co Waterford)

"Open your eyes: rugby league is not your enemy"

THE PETITION

Now for my reply to The Times:

Dear Sir,

There has been a media petition circulating in the game of rugby league deploring the constant trashing of the sport by certain media outlets. League fans can accept constructive criticism, but not over the top articles. The petition has now reached 25,000 signatories and will be presented to Parliament some time in the future.

After writing a letter to the "Sunday Times", Alex Butler, the Sports Editor, had the courtesy to reply. However, he didn't think that the media were 'attacking rugby league'. The evidence collected suggests otherwise.

Following on from the Rugby League Grand Final, incidentally attended by over 60,000 fans with a strong representation of families and children, we now have the "Times" response dated 15.10.01. For your benefit I have enclosed a copy.

It has to be said that the article by Simon Barnes has won your paper the 'Golden Boot' award. Boot as in up the backside. I have read some appalling press coverage this year but yours takes the biscuit.

One can only guess that it was spewed out whilst under the influence of alcohol. It can't be decided if it should be framed or used for the toilet.

Up here in the outback, we second class-citizens have what are called 'car boot' sales. Although the goods would not match Harrods finest, they are still worth a visit. On a recent trip, I came across some tacky picture frames, unbecoming of the sale. I feel these frames would suit your equally tatty piece of journalism. This appears to be the best option, as one can have a good laugh at night once the anger has subsided. In any event, my toilet is pure class and would shrink at the thought of such trash being put down it.

An apology doesn't seem appropriate, as any paper allowing this cannot be sincere.

I'm sorry to be so rude, which is normally against my mild manner, but for once it is bloody well meant.
Yours Sincerely,
Ray Gent

THE PETITION

Gloryhunter's Response

True to form, there is always someone from rugby league who has the wit to reply. Such is gloryhunter, a Bradford fan, who frequents the Saints message board. Here is his "Transcript of an apology from the Chief Examiner, National "A" Level Inspection Board, dated 30th August 2050.":

As a result of the inaccurate and confusing wording of the preamble to the question headed "Final that signalled the beginning of the end", I have reluctantly decided that the papers submitted by all Sports Studies students this year should be declared null and void, and that all candidates for the "A" level exam should be invited to resit.

This is obviously a very serious step, but after careful consideration of the facts I believe I have no alternative.

Whilst the preamble correctly identified the merging of the two rugby codes, serious omissions were made in the summary of events that led up to this momentous point in sporting history. In particular, the failure to mention the abolition by the RFU in 2007 of the 'line out' and the 'rolling maul', and adoption of the 'play the ball' and six-tackle rule by rugby union (in 2010) was a serious mistake. Perhaps worst of all, there was no mention of the critical decision by the RFU in 2012 to reduce the number of players in a team to thirteen, plus four substitutes, and to change the points scoring system to match that of rugby league.

These glaring omissions from the preamble were reinforced by several lesser ones, including the failure to mention the famous 'Just because you haven't got any decent half backs of your own' scandal surrounding the selection of New Zealander Henry Paul for England before he had ever trained with his union club. Last, but not least, the failure to include any mention of the fact that the Zurich Premiership had been won only by clubs from the old Super League whilst none from the old union clubs had been successful between the years 2015 and the present day was seriously misleading.

I believe that the pass rate of 1.5% in this exam is due in no small part to the indisputable fact that students were confused by this question, and came to believe that rugby union had superseded rugby league, whereas, as all serious historians know, the opposite was the case.

I therefore apologise to all students and their families for the situation we find ourselves in, and I assure them that rigorous efforts will be made to ensure the accuracy of the replacement examination.

The author of the erroneous preamble, Mr. Simon Barnes, has been suspended from duty pending his successful completion of a dissertation on "Journalism - A Search for the Truth".

Proof of the Pudding

Whilst talking to Geoff Lee, author of 'One Winter', he mentioned that he had had an interesting night collecting petition signatures. Here are Geoff's views as told on the www.rlfans.com web page:

"Last night, I stood outside the Pennington's Variety club in Bradford asking for petition signatures from the Bulls' fans as they were queuing to get into their club's Players' Awards evening.

THE PETITION

I was amazed at just how many had already signed it, and many of those who hadn't immediately indicated their support for it.

It was quite a pleasant way to spend an hour; I even managed to meet one of the site's regular contributors, Bully Bully no less, and collected around 300 signatures. However, right at the end of the queue were two couples that refused, although on what grounds I do not know.

No doubt if one of the anti-rugby league journalists had been with me he would have carried the story into his paper and he would have probably used the incident as proof that support for the Fans' Media Petition was now crumbling right across the north of England."

SIGN ONLINE COMMENT
(Fan in London)

"Rugby league for life. East London born and bred, as are my family. No affiliation to rugby league, that was until I saw my first game ten years ago. I've played the game and love it"

10

Ashes to Ashes

Now for some good news at last. The Aussie tour, which was cancelled, is now back on again but only the Test matches are to be played. This about turn was due to public demand not to cave in to terrorism. This will now give us a chance to see if the petition can hit 30,000 signatories. This new target, if achieved, would be some response from rugby league fans. It also appears that Maurice Lindsay brokered the deal to persuade the Aussies to do a u-turn. Although our views differ on media coverage, it is still a fantastic feat for him.

Once again it's time speak to the local media to drum up some more coverage. There is already an interview on Radio Merseyside to be done, as well as more information going into the local press. Likewise, many messages have gone onto the message boards to encourage fans to get out and collect some signatures.

All in all, it is nearly over and Parliament waits. There is a meeting to attend to, which will cover organising the petition handover. This will involve lots of work over the coming weeks. For now, it is time to see how many other contributors' hand in their written items.

Back with a Bang

Nothing is ever straightforward in rugby league. It always seems to embroil itself in controversy. The Aussie tour was cancelled and now is back on again as above. Ian Wooldridge of the "Daily Mail" had an article in his paper on the day of the Grand Final: "Why my faith in Australian manhood has been shaken" came the striking headline. Can't argue with this one as many league fans were appalled at the tour being cancelled. I just hope that if other sports do the same, then they get the same treatment.

It did take the gloss off the same paper's pre-match coverage of the Grand Final as the game produced an attendance of 60,000. I wonder why on Grand Final day he chose to focus on a negative story?

SIGN ONLINE COMMENT
(fan in York)

"Totally fed up with national media's poor treatment of rugby league. League fans pay their licence fees and buy the papers the same as other sports fans, but then have to put up with ridicule and dismissive attitudes against their chosen sport. Judging by the wide spread of locations that these comments are coming from it suggests that the game is far from dying, as media sources claim."

Testing the Water

As an exercise it was decided to post two topics on rugby league message boards to see what the papers had to say about the forthcoming Test match between Great Britain and Australia to be played on Sunday, 11th November. The ball started to roll on Sunday, 4th November. This would give some indication of events to follow.

THE PETITION

Sunday

I started with the "Sunday Mirror", and gave it 6 out of 10. There was an article of around 400 words, plus two tickets to be won. The only letdown was that the article was predominantly about one player, Gary Connolly. It also had to mention that he would soon become a rugby union player in the footsteps of Henry Paul and Jason Robinson.

There was a small article in the "Sunday People" about Adrian Morley's x-rays not arriving in Sydney. His club was waiting to see if he was fit to play in the Test match and the text highlighted this.

The "Sunday Express" and "Mail on Sunday" scored a blank, whilst the "Observer" had a minute article, 4 inches x 4 inches, tucked under 'sports politics'. It was reiterated in the "Sunday Express" that the-long term viability of league would suffer with the likes of Harris and Paul changing codes.

Excellent article by the "Sunday Times", well written and researched. In a personal letter, Alex Butler did say the "Sunday Times" was going to improve rugby league coverage, and, true to his word, he has carried it out.

Excellent article from "The Independent", whilst the "News of the World" had a small article on Andy Goodway (ex League man) going to Bath RFC club as defensive coach.

Monday

The "Daily Telegraph" mentions a scorching try by Steve Booth, ex-league player, whilst playing union. It says if he is not careful he could soon be following his more illustrious converts, Jason Robinson and Henry Paul, into the England team, yet no league coverage.

Frank Keating of "The Guardian" says: "Two day Test trial of the century, winner takes all; Saturday England versus Australia at rugby union; Sunday, Great Britain versus Australia at rugby league. Never a better chance for the world to watch both codes and pronounce which game is the better. Same journalist who this year predicted the death of league. I wonder which side he is on? "The Guardian" did have 6.5 pages devoted to union.

The "Daily Express", the "Daily Mail", "The Independent", "The Mirror", "The Sun" and "Daily Star" all had blanks.

Tuesday

Very good article in "The Independent". Colin Welland has a right go at some of the press for the way they treat rugby league. He can't fathom out why some ex-rugby league players are suddenly world class just because they have joined the game of rugby union, whilst when they were in league they hardly got a whisper. the "Daily Mail" had a small column next to a large article on union.

Nothing to report in the "Daily Star", "The Sun" or "The Guardian", whilst a couple of paragraphs in the "Daily Express" and "The Mirror".

Wednesday

"The Independent" had a 25-inch column, small articles in the "Daily Mail" and "The Guardian", whilst nothing in the "The Sun". The "Daily Star" had a 1-inch x 4-inch piece, whilst union's 'Errol Flynn' proportions dwarfed the "Daily Telegraph" 5-inch piece. The "Daily Express", by all accounts, had a good article, whilst "The Mirror" had a half page. The "Hull Daily Mail" had an excellent 8-page pull out all about the Test match.

THE PETITION

Thursday

Big improvement in "The Guardian", "Daily Star" and "TheSun".
Half a page in the "Daily Express", full page in the London "Metro",
whilst "sportinglife.com" had a very good article saying league is not
dying.

Two good articles in "The Independent", whilst "The Mirror"
had a third of a page. There was a quarter of a page on league in the
"Daily Mail", whilst union had one and three quarters.

Friday

Once again "The Independent" shines through with two good arti-
cles. There is half a page in the "Daily Star", quarter page in "The
Mirror", half page in the "Daily Express" and two columns in "The
Guardian". Better in the "Daily Mail" with a large article.

All in all, it has been a mixed week regards the press coverage.
There have been some notable articles, others at half-way house,
whilst a few were tucked away in an obscure corner. It wouldn't be
rugby league without the customary snipes, whilst some papers had
an exclusion zone sign, especially in some of the Sunday editions.

1895 Club

It was interesting to listen to comments at the re-birth of the '1895
Club' held at the famous George Hotel in Huddersfield the day
before the first Test match in 2001.

David Hinchliffe MP, who does some sterling work for rugby
league, reiterated that the game needs one Chief Executive to lead it
forward. Being disjointed cannot help our profile in terms of the
media. After all, there are always those journalists who love nothing
better than to spread the negatives. He went on to suggest that our

game is community based, rather than corporate, and we should use this strength to gain some ground in opinion.

Terry Wynn MEP, another fighter for our cause, was also critical of the game's leadership. He felt we could hardly point the finger at other sports for discrimination, when, in fact, our game sometimes doesn't help matters with the in-house fighting, and squabbles about what organisation players should belong to. He did promise to write a piece for the book, which, if forthcoming due to time scale, will be included.

Dave Hadfield of "The Independent" was critical of the events leading up to the first Test. Apparently, the Great Britain coach, David Waite, had placed his players in 'chains', as they were barred from giving press interviews. It was only after exerting pressure that matters were resolved. It is always important to at least have some players available to interview, so the game can be placed in the 'shop window'. No use having a go at the press if the sport can't oblige them with 'copy'.

All agreed that the game needs consistency at international level. Irregular Tours and Test matches do nothing to enhance the sport's image. Mention was made of the urgent need to have in place a high profile Chief Executive who will lead from the front. Sky TV was commended for its splendid coverage, but it was reiterated that our sport also needs terrestrial TV.

Testing Time

The first Test has come and gone, and first blood to the British lads, 20 point to 12. Still two more Tests to go, so no counting of any chickens. It was disappointing that the match couldn't quite make a full house, the attendance just falling short of capacity by 2,000, and the official attendance being announced as 21,758.

Now what of the papers from information gathered from the various message boards? The game hit the back page of "The Mirror", plus one and a half pages inside. "The Independent" had a full page on the front of the sports section, as did "The Times". "The Sun" had a small picture on the back plus a good write-up, whilst the "Daily Telegraph" had the report on the back page. One full page inside for the "Daily Express", and two thirds for the the "Daily Mail", plus small picture on the back. As for "The Guardian", they gave it some massive coverage as well.

From the above, there were one or two minor digs at the game and league in general, but they can be forgiven this time. Welcome back international Rugby League, and well done the press. Time will tell if this is a turning of the tide, or just an Indian summer.

Now what of Gary Hetherington of Leeds RLFC, director of Super League (Europe), and also a leading figure of the Leeds Tykes? Someone from one of the internet message boards said that he heard him on a radio interview at the Tykes versus Leicester union match at the same time as the league international. Wonder what Mr. Hetherington's views are on international Rugby League?

The Publicity Machine grinds to a halt

It's now time to sell tickets for the next Test, and so for the RFL it's all systems go, that is, if the systems are operative. It appears that the ticket phone lines have crashed. Fans may as well have been stranded in the Sahara desert as trying to order tickets. Irate callers complained bitterly of not being able to get through all day. No matter who is responsible, it is still another bullet in the foot.

Paul Cunliffe of the RLSA has given an interesting insight regarding an offer to the RFL to restore their website for free. The RLSA, along with other people, had offered help to run the website for over a year. Their assistance would have dragged the outdated system into the 21st Century.

He makes the valid point that, at the forefront of any marketing strategy, it is important to understand market awareness and to know to whom you are selling your products.

The offer included adding online merchandising and ticket sales, audio and video snaps and interviews. Also included would be supporter and press mailing lists, so that the RFL could have easy access to customers for their products.

After attending a meeting to discuss the above, there were two points that came out. After reiterating that a new, updated website would add value in being able to sell more merchandise, this was the reply from a senior executive:

"…but, we have nothing to sell!"

The second, less pertinent, point was that after traipsing over to Red Hall in Leeds on a Wednesday morning, having taken the whole day off, it was then a let-down to be told that they had four companies whom they were going to pay in excess of five figures to produce the website, and, in fact, the executive could only part with 40 minutes anyway. Clearly he was under huge pressure to go away and sell 'nothing' for the rest of the day, which takes up lots of time as everyone knows.

In contrast, Paul subscribed to the rugby union press list two weeks prior to the league Ashes Test series. There were two union games to be played, one against Australia and another against Romania in successive weeks.

In all, 15 press releases were received from the RFU regarding their forthcoming friendlies, and, sure enough, this information all ended in the papers. In contrast, only two press releases were received from the RFL up to the Friday before the first league Test. One contained the information that the Aussie team had arrived, the other what time the first press conference was.

On the actual Friday, seven press releases were then received in one go from the RFL. The next day some of them hit the daily papers, but three or four press releases are needed every day to keep a good flow of 'copy' to the papers.

Paul concludes that, until we get our house in order in rugby league, we will always attract unsavoury comment. Clearly, however, the constant scandalous accusations that our game is dying are way off the mark and we would be much happier to read constructive criticism.

Finally, the Ashes we play for are not the ashes of our game, nor will they ever be. The dust will settle, but until we drop the tag of "the Ratners of world sport" by completely and fundamentally changing the attitude of those who run our game, we will always be an easy target for the national daily newspapers.

Footnote

A letter was sent to the RFL to see what press releases were given to the Sunday papers the week prior to the first Test. This was done after the 'testing the water' mentioned previously resulted in little publicity. As of the last Test, there has been no reply. Could be they have been busy with the Test match? If an answer is forthcoming it will be included here. Watch this space…(but not for too long!)

Back to the Drawing Board

Normal service resumed after the first Test win. The second Test ended Great Britain 12 points, Australia 40. Two late converted tries by Britain gave it some respectability. As for the attendance of around 22,000, this was poor. No marketing, high ticket prices, problems obtaining tickets, fans' apathy for internationals! The bottom line is that it is still poor for an international. Just over 6,000 more than attended the Saints versus Brisbane World Challenge.

When we have Super League telling us that our game's strength is in the club game, then I can only despair. It's going to take a brave person to even contemplate using a larger stadium in the future.

THE PETITION

Test-ing Time

The third Test is now over with a win for the Aussies 28 to 8. It was a brave effort from the Britain team, and only for two disallowed tries it could have been different. Mr. Harrigan, the Aussie referee decided to court the video ref twice after being criticized in Australia for not doing so.

As for the Aussie water carriers, they were a disgrace on a chilly November evening. They must have spent 85% of the match on the field of play to coach their team. They certainly laughed in the face of Mr. McCallum of the RFL, who had in the week previous to the match sent warnings out specifically against this. It truly spoiled a great occasion.

The ticketing problems, coupled with the debacle over who should referee the third Test, has certainly left the RFL with many question marks against its name. The actual referee problem had over a third of a page devoted to it in a national newspaper, as well as a Sky TV commentator laughing his head off. The actual referee dispute was because both countries wanted their own referee. Finally it was decided by a draw out of a hat, hence the criticism, and justifiably so.

Certain media outlets have been criticised within the book, and rightly so; however, this game of ours does need a kick up the backside at times.

At least the Test match produced a sell out crowd

Glancing through a post on a message board I came across an irritated fan. Apparently the fan bought the "Sunday Times" for some coverage of the match only to find nothing. The fan went on to say the excuse was that the game kicked off at 7 o'clock. This is an interesting situation as we are told that Friday league games should kick off at 7.30pm so that they can go into the papers next day. What a let down after the paper had offered some good articles. I hasten to add, the paper did include five pages of rugby union!

As for "The Independent", "Sunday People", "Mail on Sunday", "The Observer", "Sunday Express" and "News of the World", they all had a match report. Well done to the "Sunday Mirror" who had a page and a half of league, whilst union had a half page. Without being disrespectful to union, it's a nice reversal of coverage. A congratulatory letter winged its way to the Sunday Mirror.

The "News of the World" had a column devoted to the fact that the league game was £1.5 million in debt, and to the fact that the outgoing Chairman of the RFL, Sir Rodney Walker, had requested the paper not to publish the fact. The "News of the World", being the "News of the World", thought differently.

A letter will go to them to see if the article was positive constructive criticism done in good faith, or just as another propaganda piece. Again, watch this space for a reply....

THE PETITION

That was the editor of the newspaper

I was trying to explain the importance of positive coverage in the papers

Was it a bad connection

It's always difficult to talk to narrow minded people like that

!

11

Onwards and Upwards

At the time of writing, December 2001, the petition is now closed at 30000 signatories, wildly above expectations.

The bulk of the collecting was done by only a handful of people, in some ways a tribute to those that got involved, but in other ways if every fan had got one sheet of 25 signatures each, the sky would have been the limit. Still, even only as a sample of potential support, 30,000 votes would elect an MP.

The petition's presentation to Parliament now needs scheduling, via our "'friend in high places", David Hinchliffe MP. Time and opportunity are limited and we are to some extent in the hands of others as to when this happens.

Together with the signatures there will be a presentation document (published at the back of this book as an appendix), which makes interesting reading in itself. It includes some notable signatories and findings which arose out of contact with 30,000 people. The presentation document itself will be circulated to a great many media organisations, some friendly, some indifferent and some hostile.

Whether they wish to take account of our 'opinion poll' of support for the petition's sentiments is up to them, but if sales of national newspapers continue to dwindle, especially in the rugby league heartland areas, no one can complain that they weren't told.

After all this progress, the whole subject cannot be left to drop and this book will help keep the pot boiling.

Various organisations are getting organised into carrying the 'fair media' torch, but presenting a fragmented front runs the risk of the message being diluted. However, sometimes picking up the ball and running with it gets the result without waiting for the committee to scrum down.

The 1895 group has a stance on media affairs as individuals as well as the Rugby League Supporters Association. TotalRL.com has an internet forum where this subject can be discussed and plots hatched. The RL 'trade press' routinely highlights examples of media mistreatment, and vents its outrage, but there it ends.

Organised committees do have a tendency to progress at the rate of the slowest member, so even though they are very important there is room for future activities of the 'guerrilla' type, for example further co-ordinated letter or email bombardments (some congratulatory or positive, where appropriate) of media organisations.

Whilst signing one or two people have naturally asked the sceptical question: "Aren't' you just being too sensitiv?'". The following few chapters, some by notable authors, some by ordinary fans, is a small sample of the type of support this movement has attracted and the reason why the struggle for a fair crack of the whip is justified, and needs to be carried on.

Any volunteers?"

Tim Wilkinson

12

Harry Edgar opens up on Rugby

There was a mention of the '1895 Club' on a previous page. I do believe that the new version will not be as controversial as its predecessor, with it being more of a way to promote international goodwill amongst rugby league playing nations.

During the period of the old club, Harry Edgar, a name well known in league circles was about to embark on the 'Open Rugby' magazine. This new magazine was to be dedicated to the game of rugby league. From its humble beginning, it went on to become world-famous within rugby league circles. It was eventually taken over by the same group that publishes Rugby League Express.

After making contact with Harry to reminisce, a request was made for Harry to write a piece for the book, as well as gaining permission to re-print details of the first issue of Open Rugby for entry into the book. See how matters are much the same at international level some 27 years later:

From Harry Edgar - the man behind the original "Open Rugby" magazine:

It is over a quarter of a century ago that the first issue of 'Open Rugby' magazine was born out of the same feelings and frustrations that I'm sure compelled Ray Gent to undertake his petition.

In that first issue - in the very first paragraph ever written in the magazine - I made the comment that, whilst rugby league couldn't be beaten as a sport on the field, off the field "it has suffered from such an appalling lack of good publicity it is still a minority sport in most parts of the world - it has suffered from a smear campaign by a few sick-minded patrons of a rival rugby code, and it has suffered from its own ability to promote its own assets."

Many things have come and gone, and many things have changed in the world of both codes, since I penned those words in May 1976. But not enough has changed to prevent Ray Gent and many thousands of other people still believing that their petition was needed right here in the year 2001.

On numerous occasions over the past 25 years I have written editorials in which I use the expressions "standing up for rugby league" or "defending rugby league". I wish I had not felt the need to write them, and that our game had been free to get on with its business of providing sporting entertainment for its many followers. But it wasn't - and I always felt I was speaking up on behalf of every rugby league fan and player when I attempted to put arguments from our side of the fence to counter the reams of unchallenged misinformation and deeply prejudiced opinions which have appeared all too often in some national media outlets.

In years gone by, a lot of the misrepresentation of rugby league in national media circles could be put down sheer ignorance of fact as much as any deliberate attempt to damage our game. But nobody can deny that there has been, and still is, a smug and smarmy bigotry in some people with a vested interest in rugby union who still - despite their own sport's headlong rush into professionalism and its desire to snap up as much expertise from rugby league as it can - can't help themselves when it comes to the twisting of the knife into our game.

It would be nice to think that all this sort of antagonism was dead and buried. The so-called 'war' between the two rugby codes - so often referred to in the media - has always been a totally one-sided

OPEN RUGBY

A BI-MONTHLY NEWS-SHEET OF COMMENT & OPINION FOR ALL RUGBY LEAGUE PEOPLE

Introduction

Rugby League is, we believe, the finest game there is. On the field of play it can't be beat, but off the field it has suffered from such an appalling lack of good publicity, it is still a minority sport in most parts of the world. It has suffered from a smear campaign by a few sink-minded patrons of a rival rugby code, and it has suffered from its own inability to promote its own assets.

It's time we people who know and care about Rugby League, its history and traditions, started doing more to put our game in its rightful position. It is a great injustice that our many outstanding players have not been given the widespread praise and recognition they deserve as British sportsmen. In particular, our British Lions who have battled so bravely down against the highly-trained, highly-paid Australians, only to be tragically ignored by all but a small dedicated corner of the news-media.

Sure, we want to bring Rugby League to the people. It has no pretensions, it is 'open' rugby, hence the title of this news-sheet, which we hope can play a useful role in helping the promotion and development of the game at all levels. Our aim is to provide intelligent reading for all people who care about rugby. Our emphasis will be on opinion and comment; some readers may disagree with some things we say, but believe me, we have only the interests of the game at heart.

TOURS SHOULD STAY

I am a great believer in preserving the traditions of Rugby and of the international scene, anything should come before a Test Series between Great Britain and Australia.

There has been such a lot of chopping and changing in recent times. We seem to have lost sight of the importance of having a settled pattern of international fixtures and Test matches. Not only would a definite programme of international fixtures provide more opportunity for well-planned publicity and advertising, and therefore keep the sport in the public-eye, it would also prove a great incentive for players if they could look forward to a tour every few years, or a Test Series almost every year. At the moment, the average few British players could tell you when the next international match is!

Obviously, R.L. affairs must be well planned and then arranged to settle into a set pattern of routine, so that supporters can have some definite idea of what happens.

I think we should get back to one set cycle of tours. Once every four years the Kangaroos came to Europe and Great Britain goes to Australia, and then four-year cycle the French should go "down-under" and the New Zealanders tour Europe.

There is no doubt in my mind that the Kangaroo tour of Britain could be a financial success, apart from the certainty, with such a venture should it has. Of course there must be some repeat of the achieved fixture planning that marred our 1973 tour.

A tour of games against the ten best supporters clubs in the League, plus a visit to Cumberland and a game against the Welsh, not forgetting the three Test Matches, could be an attractive, yet serious preparation within the framework of the shorter season that present day attitudes demand.

And members of a game with the Welsh raises another important issue in the international R.L. scene. The shortage of top-class players from Wales in the game today means that it is almost impossible to keep the Welsh national team on a par with the English. Test Match stands on its own.

There is still some potential interest in the Rugby League in the valleys, but the Welsh are nationals. They are die-hard rugby fans, who will not stand for the kind of cheap image R.U. television managers portray in their Rugby League coverage.

affair. Rugby league never had any axe to grind with rugby union, it never attempted to stop it being played in certain schools, educational establishments or the armed forces, and it never banned any man for playing the other code. All we ever wanted was just to be free and get on with our game.

But this never seems to be mentioned in all those newspaper columns and radio programmes, which, in recent times, have taken great delight in trying to kick when it is perceived to be down. The lack of balance in national media coverage, especially in most broadsheet newspapers, has shown no signs of abating and the propaganda machine has gone on into overdrive in recent times as union began to recruit more and more players from league.

For an 'establishment' which still cannot identify in any way with a blue collar sport like rugby league born out of the needs of working men in the north of England, our game continues to be seen only in terms of its relationship or comparison with rugby union, the ultimate 'establishment' game. They just can't get their heads around the fact that we are a totally different sport, played at many different levels by different people - both professional and amateur.

Why those broadsheet newspapers seem keen to promote rugby union and give it acres of space and sycophantic coverage way in excess of public interest when compared to even what soccer used to has almost everything to do with the old British class system. Now, it has more to do with money - the pursuit of a designer lifestyle that hits all the so-called A's and B's that the advertising agencies love. Poor old rugby league has no chance of swimming against this particular tide. For many years neither did soccer, despite its overwhelming presence as our national sport. Compared to rugby union, rugby league may have had all the honesty on its side, but that doesn't matter a fig in a society and its media where advertising money talks.

But now things have changed in many areas and our game of league can't complain too much because we've brought so many of our problems on ourselves. The lack of knowledge of what rugby league is really about has constantly manifested itself in the way the media has derided our game suggesting it has failed; on the contrary it is our game that has been failed by those who run it. So many of rugby league's wounds have been self-inflicted - never more so than in the six years since Super League turned the game on its head - and for so long the first world war expression about "lions being led by donkeys" has run true for our beloved game.

Quite simply, we have given those critics in the media who want to stick the boot in absolutely all the ammunition they need to do so - and more. And now rugby league is paying the price for its failure to challenge media myths and prejudices in years gone by, so that now almost everything goes against our game, which seems to be the dog that has become trendy for everyone to kick.

This does not stop any rugby league fan enjoying their game, or stop them wanting to stand up for it whenever they see another example of unfair treatment. What it has stopped many rugby league fans doing is buying a broadsheet newspaper, particularly on Sundays. That in itself is unfair... why should one section of society be denied the opportunity to enjoy the quality newspapers and all therein without seeing the sport they love at its best ignored, or at worst insulted and derided amid heaps of often quite blatant misinformation.

I'm sure Rupert Murdoch and other media tycoons aren't losing any sleep over the fact that so many people have turned their backs on their particular newspapers because of this. I'm sure they also won't lose too much sleep over this petition - no matter how many tens of thousands of people sign it and support it. Rupert himself might understand a little more about the passions that drive rugby league people since his famous run-in with Rabbitohs of South Sydney, but it's a dead-cert all those advertising agency minions and bankers who control the flocks at Twickenham in the pursuit of the colour supplement lifestyles the same newspapers portray, still won't have a clue why we are so angry.

But that doesn't mean we don't have to stop trying to right a wrong. This petition is an illustration of just how aggrieved so many thousands of people feel. Over the years, many fine rugby league writers have stood up for our game in the face of such overwhelming odds - men like Stanley Chadwick, 'Casca', Tom Longworth, Jack McNamara and Paul Fitzpatrick. I'm just so happy that for many years 'Open Rugby' magazine was able to do its best to defend our game as well, and lend some comfort to those many fine and brave people out there in the field battling prejudice and bigotry.

The amount of words given to our game in the national media may be a fraction compared to the other code, but one word of truth is worth a thousand of those peddling the same old misinformation from people jumping on a familiar bandwagon.

Harry Edgar

Harry, who is now a director of Whitehaven Rugby League Football Club, has now endorsed the petition on behalf of the club.

WHITEHAVEN RUGBY LEAGUE FOOTBALL CLUB

The Whitehaven club is pleased to support the petition demanding more fairness in media coverage of our sport. We know this is an issue of great concern to our supporters, just as it is to all rugby league fans around the world.

Our club and the sport as a whole enjoys excellent and much appreciated coverage from the local media, just the same as every other club in traditional rugby league areas where the game means so much to our communities. But on a national level we recognise how damaging it is to our sport to see it constantly undermined in some areas of the media. Nobody can quantify exactly how much damage the spin off from this hurts clubs like us, in terms of hitting supporter morale and sponsorship confidence in rugby league.

But certainly here in Whitehaven it just makes us doubly determined to work harder to keep the flag flying for rugby league.

All supporters who share our love of the game will always be made welcome at Whitehaven, and wish the petition every success.

SIGN ONLINE COMMENT
(fan from Wrexham)

"All we ask is for is a fair representation by newspapers, TV and other forms of media."

13

Lord Hoyle of Warrington's View

The vast majority of rugby league supporters would agree that when it comes to relationships with the media, we fare pretty poorly.

All too often, we see negative headlines, or even more worrying, no headlines at all regarding rugby league. Compare this to such sports as rugby union, football or cricket, which receive extensive coverage both in newspapers and on television.

The ongoing saga of rugby league players moving to rugby union is a classic example of the way in which rugby league is treated by the press. This issue is reported as a crisis for rugby league and a sign of rugby union's dominance over league. However, surely it is rugby union which has a problem given that they are seeking to sign rugby league stars.

Why do they need our top players? What does this say about present rugby union standards? Does this not say that that their junior development has failed over the years that they need rugby league players, both at club and international level.

While a handful of players have switched codes other top league players, such as Kris Radlinski and Keiron Cunningham, have pledged their future to league despite the interests of rugby union clubs.

So there is little doubt that there is an inherent bias against rugby league in the media. This bias may come from the traditional north/south divide and the strongest argument for a Super League club in London is that the London-based media may begin to take the game more seriously. However, this largely depends on their success and the ability to attract crowds. As yet this has not happened.

The game has also not helped itself in terms of receiving positive media coverage and we have to learn from our past mistakes. The Strategic Review has taken place and hopefully it will create a competition which attracts interest combined with high profile Test matches and a World Club play off, appealing to fans and media alike.

As mentioned above, we face a very critical media but we must not despair. There are many successes in rugby league. The amateur game continues to spread throughout the country and if we are to see the game develop in new areas it has to be based on strong grass roots support. More and more interest is being taken in the game from all over the country and with more people playing rugby league at junior and amateur level the healthier our game will be in the future.

Also, there have been significant strides made in the number of armed services personnel playing the game. This has already gone some way in breaking down the class barriers within rugby league and I hope that more military personnel play the game and provide effective competition at the amateur level.

At Super League the Grand Finals over the last four years have produced exciting matches and huge crowds have turned up of 42,000, 51,000, 58,000 and 60,000 respectively.

We do face an uphill battle in terms of attracting more favourable and extensive media coverage but I believe the game can help itself in any ways. Journalists like to knock our game and we have to prove to them that rugby league is exciting, is in a healthy state of affairs and deserves better treatment from the national media. Time will tell whether this can be achieved.

Thanks goes to Lord Hoyle for his comments. I believe that we as a sport have to get our act together, as well as the media not treating the game and its fans as second-class citizens. As the petition wording says: "We are not against constructive criticism."

SIGN ONLINE COMMENT
(fan from Chippenham, Wilts)

"Just look at the geographical spread of signatories."

14

View from the Terrace

Although the petition had its birth on the Saints message board, it is all about the rugby league family, and therefore a post was placed on various message boards by John Dotters to seek fans views on events, trying to obtain as wide a perspective as possible. Below is a selection of fans' comments.

****

(Pilchard) a Wakefield fan

My first reaction to the petition, when approached at our home match with the Saints, was "fat chance", quickly followed by, "If I don't sign, no chance". And while signing and afterwards, I realised that this is more than a mis-represented game, these are mis-represented people, and it's about time the people who print our papers give ALL their readers coverage of our interests, whatever they be, warts and all in a constructive manner.

This got me thinking about the right of might, and how, with the various communication tools at our disposal, change could be brought about by boycotting, mailing publications etc. I am so pleased to see it has grown as it did, and appreciate the amazing amount of effort and resources put in by the originator starting to approach fruition.

And can I say it, along with many things this season, set my spark alight with regards to this great game and its family. As a relative new-comer to it all, I feel the bigger audience needs to be aware of it, all the prejudices that have been heaped upon it, and the dignity with which the terrace fans have carried it off.

****

(Stukielty) a Halifax fan

The media bias is as unpalatable as it is sinister. The particular incident I remember was during the British Lions rugby union tour. There was an article in the "Sun" about Jason Robinson, and it had the following title: "At Wigan I sank 20 pints, and now I am ready to sink the Aussies." The article was an example of gutter tabloid journalism, and through a lack of fact and sheer manipulation of the truth, implied that, while at Wigan RLFC, Robinson was an alcoholic, then passed over to union where he gave up drinking and found God. We all know that is nonsense, but it represents a kind of subtle racism against groups of people bound together by their love of a game. I'd say it was a form of racism against the working class, but I think that would be giving the "Sun journalists" too much credit. They are people just expressing stupid opinions without knowledge, fairness or understanding.

****

(DonnyRhino) a Leeds fan

When we decided to play three Test matches in three small stadia along the M62 corridor, we were automatically accepting rugby league as a small northern dominated sport. If the Rugby Football League had decided to play tests at larger stadia across the country and done their utmost to fill them, then we may have been in a better bargaining position. The term "shooting yourself in the foot" springs to mind.

The product on the pitch can be outstanding, but the commercial and marketing side is an absolute shambles. The Rugby Football League and Super League do not do enough to promote the sport.

****

(pmarrow) a Hull fan

Although I helped to collect petition signatures I think our game should do more. Super League clubs to play each other only twice, some extra cup competitions and more internationals. This could boost our chances of obtaining more media coverage.

****

(conboys Mrs. C) a Hull fan

All I can say is that the petition has done nothing but good for our great game. Even if we do not get the recognition we deserve in the media at present, the petition has brought fans from different clubs together, and that HAS to be good for the game.

It has united Super League, Northern Ford Premier, Conference and school/clubs fans. Hopefully, the media will realise the potential in covering our game. If we make it a two-way partnership, it could be very beneficial for all concerned.

Through the petition this year, we have met many new friends at other clubs. We have managed to meet up and chat in person and on the message boards. It has been great to put faces to names. This would not have happened if we had not got involved with the petition.

THE PETITION

Many thanks to Ray for taking the initiative and inviting us on board. The game needs more people to take up the challenges that lie ahead. When I first read of the plans for a petition on the Saints message board I was unsure the idea would work but still enquired about the details. Having spoken to Steve, my husband, we decided to give it a go and see where it led. And here we are… Thanks to everyone who has signed and helped.

****

(Andrew F, red, amber and black) a Bradford fan

The media petition is a collective expression of the massive frustration every rugby league fan feels when reading the newspaper, watching the television or listening to the radio.

At every turn it seems, with a few honourable exceptions, the game we all support is run down, often in such a way as to present another game in a better light. And when it is not being run down, it is being ignored to a scandalous degree.

This damage is not limited to nuisance value. Media coverage indirectly bankrolls rugby union, through increasing its attractiveness to sponsors. Conversely, league has to battle against the tide - why put your logo on a player's shirt when no one outside the ground is going to see it?

Much of the excuse for this limited coverage has been league's 'limited appeal'. Yet union's appeal is very much limited to the South West and Wales, and outside that almost uniquely the middle class.

No one is asking for wall-to-wall coverage. No one is asking for people who are not fans of our game to be forced to like it. All we are looking for is for our game to be treated fairly. What justification can there be for a Scottish club rugby union game watched by an estimated 150 being given more column inches than our Grand Final watched by sixty thousand plus?

121

THE PETITION

All we want is for our sport to be given a chance. That's what the petition is about.

****

(Shaun F) a Hull FC fan

It's now over twenty years since I first tasted rugby league. I am a third generation who stood shivering with my father watching a game unfold yet couldn't understand it for some time. Many changes have altered the game irrevocably, for better or worse, richer or poorer. The game itself is - arguably - better. Definitely richer (as long as you can stay in the top echelon of the game), but the response and plaudits we get from the media are poorer. Noticeably so.

Always been irretrievably marked as a 'northern game' and seen as parochial by all those who frown on so-called 'northern pastimes'. Unfortunately it's stuck in a time warp that is perpetuated by the terrestrial channels sneering at the sport and highbrow broadsheet news comparing rugby league unfavourably with the 'other code'. To say rugby union has the lion's share of publicity is a gross understatement. It has the total share.

There are not enough people willing to give league a hefty push into the spotlight. This, in turn, blights our way forward.

The fault for our poor media-presence is difficult to pin down. Two terrestrial channels used to have whole programmes devoted to rugby league - now we are lucky to get a mention on either. In contrast, the rugby league soul was sold to an Australian media magnate seven years ago, thus giving it an audience worldwide providing you upgraded your TV, handed over your pieces of silver and bolted a large white soup-tureen to the front of your house. Now the tureen has evolved into a Jasper Conran sieve, but more homes can now have rugby league beamed at them than ever before, and that's not a bad thing.

THE PETITION

Incidentally, the contract runs out in 2002 and must be renegotiated. But by whom? Maurice Lindsay signed the first contract and looks favourite at time of writing to be the front man for the second. A collective groan shall be heard from a weary RL fan base and nervous looks will appear on the faces of club chairmen when the various executives meet to discuss how best to dissect the game further.

A portion of the blame for poor media representation lies in the first negotiation of the satellite contracts. In doing so, we committed the sport to one network and blocked access to the rest. A couple of years ago, the BBC was graciously allowed to screen 30 minutes of action from both the satellite-broadcasted games and it was packaged as a 'magazine programme'. Unfortunately, this is only carried by two BBC relays, to Yorkshire and the Granada regions. It is fronted by the token Yorkshire man and is very unprofessionally produced. It doesn't even get a mention in the TV guides.

The game has acquired many 'voices' over the decades. Some of which are difficult to shake off and they lend the sport the 'flat-cap and whippet' mentality perceived by the country. Once great players and coaches are constantly sniping at the game and its evolution, which embarrasses the sport and turns the next generation of supporters off it. They may not realise the detrimental effect their articles and interviews have, but they sound faintly ridiculous as they trot out the players of the fifties and sixties that are meaningless to the young supporters who are needed if the sport is to survive.

Mention Alan Hardisty, Roger Millward, Derek Fox and Johnny Whitely to any young Bulls fan and you will get a blank look. They may as well run round Odsal singing 'On Ilkey Moor B`aht At'. What is needed are fresh young voices fronting the game. The new players in our game with their marketable faces and looks of a surfer will win support. An insight into Bradford's revival shows the effect the Paul brothers have, with their theme songs, bronzed skin and teeth that shine like Liberace's dressing gown.

All credit to Bradford for seeing the marketing potential that football created which has revitalised their club more than Keith Mumby ever could. Their next generation of fans may not know who Bradford Northern were, but do they really need to? In football, David Beckham's football prowess is secondary to his ability to draw money as young fans rush to buy his posters, replica shirts and his wife's latest caterwauling on CD.

Who does RL have? Martin Offiah with his appearances on 'A Question Of Sport` and Adam Fogerty's silver screen bit parts. Offiah was the sports first millionaire and, I daresay, will be the only player not to own a pub near a rugby league stadium.

The other code of rugby union is seen by many as the definitive game played at University by the lawyers, politicians, stockbrokers and editors - the 'old school tie' brigade of towel-flicking hearties, debaggers, midnight feasters and square-jawed men called Lawrence. The fact is, rugby league is now played at the highest seats of learning, but the rest of the nation remains sadly unaware of its growth.

The rugby league international game is covered with a cursory regard and receives derision when the British team fails again to defeat our colonial cousins from the Southern Hemisphere. The fact that the nation's cricketers, RU players and athletes also fail miserably is discounted. All the armed forces have regular inter-service tournaments and the Summer Conference spans the country. The grass roots of rugby league are being sowed and, in many cases, are producing harvests, albeit unrecognised.

Failure by the men at the highest level of the rugby league to successfully market and package the sport is beyond belief. Conflicts of interest are rife and, to some extent, unethical. Directors and Chairmen of the most successful clubs in the country are given seats on the board of the governing body, yet only cover their own interests and forget the game's place in the grand scheme of things. Accusations of favouritism, elitism and everything bar rheumatism are thrown from all quarters with no fear of retribution.

If the game is to progress and be given recognition and kudos it must select independent bodies to oversee the game in a similar vein to the Football Association. Businessmen and people of high media profile should be sought to force awareness and keep order. Governmental sports grants seem to pass the sport by but have enabled rugby union clubs, starved of truly great talent, to wave large amounts of money in the faces of league's finest players. It's hard to resist such advances when your career is often over before you are 35 and you don't have a desire to run a pub in Leeds. No names, no pack-drill.

Hard as it is to get the game recognised and sold to a football-loving public, the media petitions and united supporters' groups have their own part to play. But do the men in charge or the powers-that-be have the same loyalty, passion and drive?

The jury are still out on that one.

****

(The Rick) a Wakefield fan

Anything that raises the profile of rugby league is a good thing in my book. League can never get away from the stigma of the 'Northern, working class game', but, frankly, I'm proud of the roots of this sport, proud of where we came from, and proud that I'm now supporting the club that my family has supported for years. I'm proud of the heritage of my club, and I'm proud to be a supporter of rugby league.

The media coverage is pretty dire, although fair play to "The Independent", probably the best for rugby league writing, but until we get our own Stephen Jones, we'll always be fighting the stories of 'Rugby League is dying'.

My chosen sport needs good news coming out on a regular basis, and the whole Keiron Cunningham affair really showed up the WRU for what they are. Just because they couldn't get their man, they smeared his character and heritage. Pretty sad for a bunch of people "superior" to us league people.

They can take away our best players, and hey, there'll always be another Harris, or Paul, or Robinson coming through. One of my ambitions is, in the future, to be a rugby league journalist, so maybe, one day; I'll be joining the fight-back!

****

(davethebull) a Bradford fan

I think the petition is a show of frustration at the way things are. How is rugby league supposed to move forward when it is constantly having its obituary written? Rugby league has a right to exist, just like any other sport. The media should recognise this and move on.

15

Green Shoots of Recovery

You can play rugby league at UNIVERSITIES? John Grime, a student at Sheffield University, stands up for league:

I arrived at Sheffield University lacking any real sporting background, but having developed a keen interest in rugby league via televised games over the previous two years. I joined the rugby league club at the first opportunity, a decision which I will never regret.

The sense of camaraderie on and off the field has been a source of constant entertainment and I am convinced that the future impact of the Student game on the sport as a whole cannot be underestimated. Anyone familiar with the details surrounding the Guinness sponsorship of the 2001 Ashes Tests will readily testify to this.

We now have our own "old boys' network." Soon, league-loving graduates will begin to assume key roles in business and the media, bringing with them access to the sponsorship and coverage so essential to any sporting endeavour. The cross-section of the population represented in the Student game will impress many of those who misguidedly stereotype rugby league as an exclusively northern, working-class sport. Recruits from across the geographical and social spectrums quickly come to love the demanding nature of league defence allied to the physical fitness and attacking instinct required to play the game effectively.

Student rugby league no longer has to rely on the hard work of a small group of enthusiasts; it has taken on its own momentum and will continue to spread the gospel throughout colleges, universities and other higher education establishments.

Today, approximately 65 teams (72 with women's teams included) make up the various university leagues and competitions. Another 24 play in the colleges, 48 establishments in all.

I suppose the turning point came in 1989, when full-time officers in Bev Risman and Malcolm Reid helped the enthusiasts plot a steady growth over the next decade. World Cups in '89, '92, '96 and '99 attracted major sponsors such as "The Independent" and the (then) "Halifax Building Society". Who could forget the sight of Dutch students in their orange clogs adding a touch of colour to the northern scene?

And who can forget the massive success of the recent European Championships in Tatarstan? The crowds in Kazan were amazing and their enthusiasm for the game inspirational. What M62 corridor?

A dying game? Try getting out a map of English counties and put in different coloured pins for college, university, school, BARLA and Conference teams. You should find all counties covered with pins. Then there's Wales, Scotland and Ireland, who are co-hosting, along with England, the Queensland Students in December.

Please back Student rugby league - it will pay back investment a hundred-fold in the future.

Alive and Well.

SIGN ONLINE COMMENT
(fan in St Helens)

"The game of rugby league is enjoyed by all members of our family from six to eighty-six. How can such a great piece of entertainment, not to mention our heritage, be so marginalised and condemned. It's a disgrace"

THE PETITION

Whilst attending the '1895 Club' meeting, I got talking to Peter Benson who helps out with the Yorkshire Junior League. He said that he would do some research on the growth of league, which does suggest that the grass roots are alive and kicking.

The league is made up of clubs from Leeds, Wakefield, Castleford, York, Doncaster and Heavy Woollen (Batley and Dewsbury). Here are the statistics:

> 1992 season: 59 clubs with 187 teams
> 1993 season: 51 clubs with 180 teams
> 1994 season: 54 clubs with 188 teams
> 1995 season: 51 clubs with 210 teams
> 1996 season: 59 clubs with 193 teams
> 1997 season: 54 clubs with 236 teams
> 1998 season: 54 clubs with 242 teams
> 1999 season: 59 clubs with 212 teams
> 2000 season: 56 clubs with 253 teams
> 2001 season: 53 clubs with 248 teams

Pretty impressive from 1992 in that there are 61 more teams despite six less clubs. The fall in teams in 1999 was due to BARLA instructing the Bradford and Halifax clubs to join the West Riding League. So on this information it seems to be one of progress in the number of junior teams participating in rugby league. Definitely no coffins here yet.

SIGN ONLINE COMMENT

"I'm sick of the bias in the national media, especially as the Summer Conference League spreads across the country even more."

16

A European View

Terry Wynn is a member of the European Parliament, as well as a member of the European group of Rugby League MP's. Terry has kindly given his views on our game and the media:

Rugby league is more than just a game, it's a belief, a way of life and, at times, it's like being part of an oppressed minority.

At the same time, rugby league can be its own worst enemy. When I finished reading Geoffrey Moorhouse's "Official History of Rugby League", I came to the conclusion that rugby league had survived 100 years in spite of itself.

When we complain about lack of press coverage, why should any editor take notice of a minority sport that excels at squabbling and has division within its ranks? RL splits wherever it is played, South Africa, Russia, Japan, Fiji, as well as the well-known rows in the UK and Australia.

How can Super League clubs expect match coverage in the national dailies when they kick off at 8pm, which ensures deadlines can't be met? Why should the national press take us seriously when we can not fill a stadium for a Test match, or when Man. United get 10 to 15% more spectators at Old Trafford than we get in total on an average weekend? In European terms, the game is played professionally along the M62 corridor plus one team in London, and at semi pro level in three counties of England, as well as in pockets of southern France.

So there are plenty of reasons for not reporting the game and, at times, we have to live with that. The interesting thing, though, is not so much the lack of coverage as the bile and vilification that pours forth from some newspapers. To ignore rugby league because of its masochistic streak is one thing, to be constantly sledging it is another matter. And the reason? Those same writers know that RL is a game of immense skill, speed, courage and handling ability but they can't admit it.

Rugby union is a fine game, loved by many, and I don't think we should spend our time criticising that game. However, the critics who would see our demise are fair targets.

Being a rugby league fan is like spreading the gospel to those who haven't yet seen it. European colleagues, who see it for the first time, love it. Many watch a game on the BBC when the Challenge Cup is played. The trouble is that RL is long on potential but short on delivery when it comes to expanding the game. And as long as it stays that way, the hostile press will continue to treat us the way they do. They want to see our demise, but, unfortunately for them, RL players are our saving grace. Whatever the problems off the field, the athletes who turn out at all levels are a credit to our game and continue to show why it is such a great sport. Because of them, some journalists are jealous of what they see and if they can't produce talent like that, then they would rather see RL disappear off the face of the earth than admit it.

It's never been any different. Rugby league has survived 106 years in spite of itself and sections of the press and will continue to do so.

Terry Wynn MEP

THE PETITION

Match? - Which Match?

By Roger Grime, an ex-schoolteacher with many trips to France under his belt.

It's not easy supporting the game of Rugby League internationally. Not because of any language problem, just that the organisers are completely and utterly incompetent.

For me, 1999 showed just how deficient our paid administrators are. After almost 30 years of organising Junior tours to France, I took the plunge and booked for the Tri-Nations. I offered it up to my wife as a Silver Wedding celebration; she, of course, saw through me immediately, but nevertheless fancied the "trip of a lifetime".

As you all remember, there weren't many problems. Just the normal "the tournament's off", then the odd switch of venue the odd couple of thousand miles to Auckland, no Final in Sydney as arranged. Little things like that.

Some people never learn. Responding to calls to support the game in France, we booked two weeks away in May 2001, one in the southern heartland to take in the local RL scene and the other close to Paris, handy for the Charlety and the French Cup Final.

After a wonderful week wandering to such places of pilgrimage as Jean Galia's birthplace in Ille-sur-Têt and searching out picturesque grounds and "siéges" (every French club has a bar somewhere in the town which serves as a meeting-point for local Treizistes), we found ourselves, on the Sunday before the game, at a junior rally in St Cyprien, southeast of Perpignan. It was very French: barbecue manned by parents bickering noisily, but amicably, over culinary techniques, invitations over the tannoy for team officials to partake of aperitifs (it was, after all, late morning) and a maelstrom of heated coaches and sulking players shouting and milling animatedly in what would pass for chaos in the UK. I loved it.

Chatting away, we mentioned how much we were looking forward to the big game in Paris next Saturday. Blank looks, then a gentle, embarrassed correction that it had been moved a mere 500 miles south to Narbonne! Gallic shrugs and plenty of "Je suis désolé, mais….."

I've found it very useful, this droop of the shoulders, lowering of the corners of the mouth and muttering and gesticulating. Something that anyone who's tried to get through on the RFL "Hot-Line" will find indispensable. It may stop you from screaming and hurling the phone in frustration at the wall. But does it help anyone to actually catch the hoped-for game? Well, no. Perhaps those unfortunates who booked on the "League Express" trip might agree.

But the thing is, a trip to France is a wonderland for the Leaguie. Pockets of the keenest supporters of the game put us to shame as we moan about people not loving us and not giving us the column inches we deserve. I know it's true, but these folk are really up against it and it's the duty of Brits to give them every last bit of assistance, even if, sometimes, it's very difficult to do.

Ah well, surely we couldn't be "done" again over the 2001 October Test? Oh yes, we could. It's not so much that, after announcing venue and date, it was switched to Friday instead of Saturday. It's not even that the new venue was 100 miles away from our long-booked accommodation, so handy for the original venue of Carcassonne. It's because it was now switched to Agen.

Now, as we all know, Agen is the fiefdom of the repulsive Albert

Ferrasse, who tried with every fibre of his conniving body to kill league in France during his Chairmanship of the Agen RU club and Presidency of the FFR (French Rugby Union).

But first, we really need to go a little further back in time. In 1934, FIRA was born -the Féderation Internationale de Rugby Amateur - composed of such enlightened parties as Mussolini's Italy, Salazar's Portugal, oh yes, and Hitler's Germany. The French Union sympathisers in this august body went on to become leading figures in the Vichy government, which is so reviled for collaborating with the Nazis and which just happened to issue the edict banning Rugby league and seizing all its assets.

Not even today, with all the compensation that has been paid out to victims of the Vichy regime, has the French Rugby League received one single franc.

But surely, once the war was over, a new spirit would prevail and Treizistes, who played such a massive role in the Resistance, would see old prejudices forgotten?

Well, as Mike Rylance relates in his excellent "The Forbidden Game", it didn't quite happen like that. He tells how all RU internationals were admitted free to the Villeneuve-Carcassonne charity game in Paris in 1944 in aid of Free French Forces still fighting in Alsace. Yet Marius Guiral, Villeneuve's full-back in that match, was later refused admission to Agen's ground despite showing his union international's card, which he had gained after being forced to return to union in 1943 when he played in Agen's championship team!

Yes, the Agen mafia were reverting to type along with the rest of the union bullyboys. In 1948, FIRA was reactivated by the French RU and took control of all the posts. Although 70 countries were technically members, only the French held office for over 50 years and our friend, Albert Ferrasse, was President. The persecution recommenced.

Closer to today, in the summer of 1995, Jacques Fouroux's summer RL competition was proving enormously popular and the final was booked for the municipal stadium at Béziers.

Two weeks before match day, the town council pulled the plug on the game as soon as the FFR blackmailed them with a threat to move an All Blacks tour game from Béziers if they allowed the league game to take place. I wonder if Agen's favourite son had anything to do with that?

Well, let's move on to November 1998. Arrangements were being finalised to stage a televised evening RL game at Agen. The Villeneuve directors had agreed details with the Agen town officials (remember this is a municipal ground), when our Albert, past Chairman of the club and ex-President of the FFR, got wind of this "sacrilege". How strange, a fax suddenly arrived from the French RU President demanding that permission for them to play be withdrawn. He felt the ground would be "soiled" by the Treizistes!

And history does repeat itself. Here we were in Agen, October 2001, supporting the efforts of the French Federation and Villeneuve Leopards in particular, when lo and behold, up pops Albert again! He pleads in the press with the people of Agen to boycott this game, which "would leave the pitch in need of decontamination".

And we thought we were up against it!

But do you know, it was a great success. There was a decent crowd of 8,000 plus and many of the Agen union supporters ignored the cretinous Ferrasse and turned out to enjoy a game of rugby and support their countrymen.

We had a marvellous time. We had turned up in Villeneuve-sur-Lot on the Sunday before the Test and met Pierre-Etienne Augros in the Leopards' HQ, Bar Regent, to collect our tickets for the loge at the Stade Armandie in Agen. Villeneuve President, Pierre Soubiran, who had worked so hard to promote the Test, was issuing orders. Everyone was bustling about in preparation for leaving for Albi for the afternoon's match in that peculiar French way - coffee, red wine and cigs.

THE PETITION

My fractured French was getting me by until one large gentleman turned and requested, "Speak bloody English, mate", and I had met the redoubtable Grant Doorey, coach and prop. He still doesn't know why he's still here instead of hometown North Sydney, but was gracious enough to compare St Helens unfavourably with both. You don't argue with someone who fills the bar and most of the pavement outside and I agreed that my birthplace might have minor deficiencies.

Finally, match day arrived. A reconnaissance was called for and Stevo and Shaun McRae knew the way. "It's just down that road." Well it was, but Agen is quite big and the stroll impacted a little on my minor gout. We decided to return in the evening by taxi. Our driver knew his rights and was determined to drive right up the closed-off road to the turnstiles, practically running down security men and hurling abuse at gendarmes before narrowly missing the terrified queue and depositing us in triumph with a final screech of brakes.

Inside, it seemed like carnival time. Raucous tents selling souvenirs; raffle tickets and exotically filled baguettes; wine stalls and heated conversations. Ray French holding court. The affable and helpful Keith Senior taking our cards for Lee Briers and Paul Wellens. Brits in their club jerseys, wandering and soaking up an atmosphere unlike anywhere else.

Bands blossomed everywhere, as sweating men lugged heavy instruments and large plastic wine containers. Crowds of kids with jerseys proudly emblazoned with small village teams: Homps, Ste Livrade and La Réole. Treizistes gathered to proclaim the faith.

We had, for once, splashed out on our tickets and found ourselves in excellent company in our loge - a box, which opened out onto the main stand. Bottles of wine stood ready and a sense of conviviality abounded. After fireworks and anthems, the first 20 minutes were an anti-climax as GB raced into a commanding lead, scoring seemingly with every bout of possession. An embarrassment was on the cards, and Rugby à Treize was about to be humiliated in "enemy" territory.

Thankfully, half time came with little further damage and our companions attacked the champagne and oysters, thrusting shell after shell and glass after glass in our direction. A drunken Parisian visited to great general hilarity and we learned that our companions were a replacement windows team from Agen and a lively group led by Eric, a manic restaurateur from Toulouse.

The second half saw France regain respect and the proceedings were declared satisfactory. Now for the post-match, where bonhomie reigned supreme and thieving of wine from neighbouring tables was considered normal. Thierry, from Foix, dragged me over to Jean-Paul Ferré's table on the pretext of attending the same Primary School as the President, and after affectionate greetings, grabbed me a huge poster off the wall as a souvenir.

Somehow, we ended up outside Eric's restaurant at 3am ("For cognac and coffee: it is normal") but he had lost his keys, and when his friends started attacking the chains on the doors with bolt-cutters, we decided that perhaps that was the best time to make our excuses. With lifetime friendships sworn, we were dropped off in Agen and tiptoed down the hotel corridor, being careful not to wake Stevo.

Of course we'll be returning next year, and I'll bet with more than the 500 or so Brits who made it to Agen. International Rugby league is the only way to raise our profile and without it, the game in France will wither further. They are hanging on in there, but what are we doing to support them? Very little. Remember how we ditched the "Treize Tournoi" which had given them hope and press credibility?

2001 is the Year of the International Revival. We go to France, the Aussies (finally) come here. Rugby union practically finances its grass roots with the proceeds of internationals, yet year after year we mess it up.

Here's a fan's ultimatum to those who consistently foul up fixtures and arrangements, who can't fill a 25,000 capacity stadium for an Ashes opener and brag about a Guinness sponsorship which just amounts to £100,000 being poured down the can because they can't even keep phone lines operating and potential customers simply give up in disgust.

Get a viable international programme going. Stop the nonsense of one-off Tests in Sydney halfway through a season and give us back our birthright. A minimum six-match tour in Australia in autumn 2003 and regular fixtures at different levels with our French allies. If you can't manage all of this, get out of our lives and let those who can, take over.

We've had enough.

Roger Grime

SIGN ONLINE COMMENT
(fan in Perpignan, France)

"Rugby league fans are united all over the world"

17

In the Service of League

Alex Service, the Saints' historian, pens a piece that starts pre war and contin-ues through to the present. It illustrates the pride we have, as well as depth of feel-ing, and questions why league and union can't live side by side.

This Great Game of Ours!

The old Grange Park School in St. Helens was opened in 1938. One year later it was starting to show signs of sporting excellence when the rugby league team won the Ellison Cup. As the War was drawing to a close, another group of youngsters lifted the Waring Cup - the first in a series of finals during school life. Norman Owen, a former pupil and member of that successful team, came to us at Broadway High School and suggested a reunion of the lads who won the first Post-War honour for the school. The former winger, nicknamed 'Quicksilver', also mentioned the fact that they got the Waring Cup itself to display at school.... But got no medals! The reason? Post-War austerity. There was a shortage of metal.

No problem! The current school agreed to provide medals for the Old Originals and they were presented at a special assembly in the Main Hall. To cut a long story short, it was a magnificent occasion. After a brilliant introduction from Norman - with their '1945' image as a backdrop - each member of the squad came out to rapturous applause from special guests and current pupils. They were genuinely 'chuffed' to be recognised in this way. For some, it was the first time they had met in over half a century.

Unfortunately, their former 'Teacher-in-Charge', Horace Davies, had passed away several years ago and the team decided to present a special memento to his son, Peter, who was equally touched by such a tremendous gesture! It is quite clear that the presentation of these medals....actually they were superb trophies.... meant as much to the lads as it would have done all those years ago. It merely emphasises what this game means to us all. It is very much part of our life - something that we have been brought up with - and hopefully will remain so!

But what of the present? What a pleasure it was to take my own Year 11 pupils to play against our old adversaries at Parr. The victory was a welcome bonus as the two sides went at each other hammer and tongs! They all came off covered with sticky, stinking mud....the wrecker of many a washing machine....yet given the total commitment of the Broadway lads, washing the kit doesn't seem like too much of a chore!

The following evening, at Liverpool St. Helens ground, the town's under 16s defeated Wigan in an absolute stormer of a match! Nip and tuck it was right to the end! My loose forward from the Parr match, Paul Leyland, was in the centre for the town and showed little sign of fatigue from the previous day's encounter, with a brilliant performance. Makes you proud to be involved in some way in this great game of ours!

What a sight Moss Lane (home of the rugby union club) was on that Wednesday evening - veritably buzzing! Apart from the two Town rugby league fixtures on show, which drew large crowds, there was also training for the parent rugby union club itself, including their girls' team! This is what I feel rugby should be all about - the two codes co-existing and thriving. As I left the ground, I defied anyone interested in sport not to have got genuine enjoyment from the match and the occasion in general.

THE PETITION

What a pity we could not have frog-marched our 'friends' from the national media to watch the Broadway assembly, the Parr mud bath and inter-town Clash of the titans - superb adverts for the Greatest Game and lynch-pins of our sporting community! Mind you....no free lunches! Aahh yes....and then on Saturday night over 60,000 packed into Old Trafford for the Grand Final between Bradford and Wigan....an attendance far superior to any Premier League football match that day. Yet a match report could only be found in moderation five or six pages back in some of our more notable nationals!

Basically, we need to keep on fighting the good fight for our code in the face of some unbelievable indifference from the media. Or is it merely indifference? On Sky's Rugby League World, Greg McCallum talked of a 'media campaign to de-stabilise rugby league' during the 2000 World Cup. Yet it still continues! Who is kidding whom? Why not bring matters into the open? Once the battle lines have been drawn we can all play our part in standing up for our game! Don't forget that we have been referred to as 'Sewer rats' in one damaging piece of cheap, tatty non-journalism....pot calling the kettle black, if you ask me!

They can call us what they like from their plush offices in London, but they will never succeed in defeating us. When cornered, rats, especially the sewer variety, have one heck of a nasty bite! Long live rugby league!

Alex Service

18

The Northern Lights

Phil Stockton lives in Aberdeen and regularly keeps in touch with his sport by internet. He frequents rugby league message boards, as well as reading articles from newspapers on the net. Not for him the joy of being able to pop round the paper shop for his weekly dose of rugby league papers; Phil has to order for the year. This is Phil's view of a grim life even further up north outside rugby league:

Living outside the heartlands gives you a different perspective on the place of rugby league in the nation's sporting psyche. I grew up in Salford where my Dad used to take me to the Willows to watch the great Salford team of the Seventies. In the heartlands, rugby league is part of the social fabric and you feel immersed in it. Up here, access to any league news is limited, especially in Aberdeen.

This might be expected, since as far as I know, the game is not played here at all. League coverage in the national press is not that great and is further diminished, or ignored, in Scottish editions of the papers.

The two main issues that have struck me since living here are the relatively low profile of league outside of the heartlands, especially in the media, and the threat that rugby union poses.

The threat from union has seemed to increase over the past few years. It appears to have the power to attract media attention and, through a web of social and business connections, the ability to generate considerable income in the form of corporate sponsorship and private investment. Essentially, because it is the sporting preserve of the private education system, rugby union does appear to be the British establishment at play. I don't subscribe to the view that it is exclusively an Upper Middle Class sport but I think it's these connections that have served the game well, sometimes at the expense of league.

For example, the ban, until recently, on the playing of league in the armed services did much to prevent the spread of our game internationally and there can be no doubt that it is union's international dimension that has contributed to its apparent ascendancy in the Nation's sporting consciousness.

In Aberdeen, I have friends who use their rugby union associations to further business contacts and events such as the Six Nations are the subject of much corporate hospitality. Indeed, I have been offered free tickets to see Scotland play in a Six Nations match myself because it was thought that I was interested in rugby - assumed to be union of course.

Many of my colleagues would describe themselves as union fans and it has to be said that there is considerable interest in the international scene. However, most of these fans will never have been to see any Scottish domestic club rugby. Football is miles ahead of any other sport as far as Aberdonians are concerned and most know next to nothing about the local union side, Aberdeen Grammar, despite the fact that they have recently been promoted to the Scottish First Division.

Even so, this semi-professional team has managed to attract a number of sponsors, their main one being Halliburton, who are the largest offshore construction firm in the world. The level of local interest is indicated by recent home attendances of 300, 850 and 980, and these crowds are not untypical of the rest of the league - the highest attendance of any match so far this 2001/02 season is 1,700 and the average is in the hundreds.

Despite poor crowds these matches are featured live on ITV's Rugby Scotsport on Saturday afternoons and indeed, at the moment, we are simultaneously treated to Heineken Cup action on BBC Grandstand. We have union on both main channels and rugby league can't even get the Super League Show transmitted nationwide, as it is supposedly of only regional interest, despite the fact that the Challenge Cup beats the Heineken Cup in the TV ratings. Something doesn't add up.

I am not suggesting that this melding of the corporate and media world with rugby union is some Machiavellian plot orchestrated by the union authorities, or that there is anything illegal about it - it's just the way that it is. But league should take note because the finances and publicity this avenue supplies to union is considerable.

I do not think union will attract spectators from league to cross the great divide, or that league will be absorbed by union, but the amount of money currently flowing into their game is frightening and they do pose a real threat in terms of denuding league of its staff and top players. It's true that rugby league has survived for over 100 years despite union's best efforts but this is the first time union has been openly professional and it is evidently unafraid to exploit and flex its new financial muscle.

So what? Good luck to rugby union some people may say. But such media presence is basically free advertising of their game and league struggles to get a look in adding to the profile of union and demoting league to the position of poor relation.

A further danger in all this is that the generic term Rugby is increasingly assumed to refer only to union. The grandly titled "World Corporate Games" were recently held in Aberdeen and one of the sports on offer was Touch Rugby. When I saw this played I was surprised to see that once a player is "touch tackled", play restarts with the tackled player playing the ball back between his legs to a team-mate whilst the defending team has to retire five metres. Once six such tackles have been completed the ball is handed over to the opposition. Sounds familiar?

Basically these guys are playing touch rugby league but the casual observer would probably assume this was a variant of union. I don't know if the RFL could actually protect the copying of its rules to ensure that the name "League" has to be associated with six tackles and the play the ball, but surely such flagrant plagiarism should be benefiting league in some way? If the sport had to be called Touch Rugby League or Touch League this would promote the name of the game into areas where it normally doesn't get played. Instead Touch Rugby is basically seen as a form of union when it is so much more obviously a version of league.

I am not blaming all our ills on rugby union because league has inflicted many of its own problems. I suppose it's as a consequence of being outside the heartlands that I see rugby league struggling in the face of competition from union and this has generated in me a strong feeling for the game at a collective level - its successes and failures produce much the same emotions that the weekly victories and losses of my team might evoke.

Union's current hype will, I feel, burst, especially when the more general sporting public realise that, with its lack of tries in competitive games at the top level, it often isn't actually that interesting to watch, whereas league at all levels consistently generates a brilliant spectacle. Ultimately, I believe that we have the superior product on the pitch.

I think rugby league needs to hold its nerve in these difficult times and keep the systems in place that generate the players, even if we do lose a few to union along the way. Our youth is the future and we must invest to keep that developing. Better to lose a few golden eggs than starve the goose that laid them.

However, league does need to improve its marketing and increase national awareness for talking to locals up here, they often confuse league with union, amazingly associating it with the Barbour set or view it stereotypically as the game played by the cloth cap and clog brigade.

Despite being starved of rugby league in the far north, Scotland has provided me with one of the finest rugby league occasions, the 1999 Challenge Cup Final played at Murrayfield. A mate who was an English union supporter and two local Aberdonian friends, who were principally football fans but were interested to see the match and have a day out in Edinburgh, accompanied me to the game.

It was a fantastic occasion, totally converting the union fan and, needless to say, we are all planning a return visit (with the addition of a few more) for the 2002 Challenge Cup Final. So perhaps with the right encouragement and marketing the advent of rugby league as a major sporting event (and one day, sport) in Scotland is not a total "pipe" dream.

Footnote from Ray Gent

Whilst on a visit to Chester I noticed a good marketing ploy by rugby union. The Cheshire version of Monopoly had a full picture of Jason Robinson in rugby union kit on the front of the box. Jason was, of course, a recent union convert from league. No doubt this is good basic marketing, something league definitely needs to sort out.

19

An Independent View
from Dave Hadfield

When Ray Gent first told me about his petition calling for fair treatment of rugby league by the national media, my first, unworthy, thought was: "Here we go again."

After all, rugby league has been complaining about being treated as a second-class citizen ever since it was the Northern Union. The pundits - especially those based in London and with a rugby union background - have been predicting our imminent demise since the first weekend of matches in 1895. Nothing has changed.

That, of course, is only partly true. After a hundred years during which the party line was to treat rugby league as some sort of perversion of the true faith, irretrievably tainted by the presence of - whisper it - money, the fashion now is to kill us with kindness.

Wonderful game, rugby league. Bring us your obscure talents like Jason Robinson and Iestyn Harris and we will turn them into shining stars. You rugby league chappies, if you behave yourselves, can be the finishing school that churns out the players for union.

We've all seen the patronising guff that flows from this attitude. "Great game, rugby league, such a shame it has to die" - and all the rest. Well, rugby league has news for them. It has no intention of rolling over and being absorbed into the big, soft folds of rugby union's under-belly.

It will continue to provide an entirely different sporting experience for its players and its spectators.

When national newspapers are guilty of particularly patronising excesses, I know they have been taken aback by the extent of the backlash. Lazy metropolitan journalism, stuff pre-written by people who in some cases don't even bother to go to the game, deserves to be thrown back in their faces.

I don't know whether a petition is the answer, but it is one indication that league still has some fire in its belly and I applaud its part in keeping that tradition alive.

Dave Hadfield, The Independent

Following on from the above, there was another article in the "Daily Mail" that needs some thought. It was written by Peter Jackson and dated 07.12.01. It stated that Dave Whelan, the man behind the JJB sports empire, Wigan Athletic football club and Wigan RLFC was about to embark on a £10m rebirth of Orrell RUFC. His ultimate aim was to take the ailing club back to the top of the union pile with the help of Maurice Lindsay.

The article was a full page and could not be ignored. It did stress that the merger theory between the two codes of rugby should be discounted but this was probably to hedge bets. 10,000 attendances are to be envisaged. It goes on to say that a meaningless union international between England and Romania attracted 60,000, whilst league's major attraction between Great Britain and Australia only attracted one third of that figure. No mention of the 'buy one get one free' ticket offer that union undertook to encourage fans to go to a union Cup Final, something league is slaughtered for when they do it.

Cross-code rugby is envisaged with, no doubt, burn-out for the players. Yet what of Radlinski, who signed a loyalty agreement to stay in league? Whelan is quoted as saying: "I see league and union getting closer together." He is also quoted as saying that: "Union is a world game. League, in the UK, is a northern game."

There is no doubt that Mr. Whelan is entitled to spend his money how he wants. Yet once again the propaganda machine is churning away. There is even a league table showing one and all how rugby union clubs are producing healthy rises in attendances. Yet in the past many nationals were reluctant to show union attendance figures. Not for the first time has the "Daily Mail" shown where its bias is.

Peter Jackson then replied to one of my letters in his column in the "Daily Mail" on 21.12.01. He described David Hinchliffe MP and the all-party parliamentary rugby league group of MP's as "a fine body of men who must surely have better things to do." What? Than represent their constituents, who play and watch rugby league? He then produced two sets of tables which prove only that despite the level of media hype for the union game, rugby league still has four of the top six best-supported rugby clubs in the country.

There is one question for all those editors who let their journalists downgrade rugby league with venom: "Are we rugby league fans your customers, and, if so, why do you treat our game the way you do?" And one message for all league fans: It's up to us all to keep the pressure on if we are ever going to rectify this injustice against our sport.

SIGN ONLINE COMMENT
(fan in Belfast)

"Totally fed up with the national media's poor treatment of rugby league. League fans pay their licence fees and buy newspapers the same as followers of other sports, but we have to put up with the ridicule and a dismissive attitude to our great game. Judging by the wide spread of locations these comments are originating from league is far from the dying game that most media sources would have you believe."

20

And Finally...

There is a letter printed below that sums up much about the media coverage. It is typical of many sent to various media outlets. Let it be a warning to many newspapers' Emily's. Rugby league fans are fast packing in buying newspapers. Is this what the editors of the nationals want? It is reproduced by kind permission of HaloMan who frequents the league message boards:

Dear Emily,

I feel I can no longer keep my feelings to myself regarding the abject failure of your sports pages in both "The Guardian" and "Observer" newspapers. They fail in their fundamental aim to keep the reader informed and the lack of insight they show defies any reasonable person's belief. Of course, I am not directing my criticism at the sports pages in general, just their woeful lack of coverage of rugby league.

During the league season we do get match reports, I admit. However one thing we do not get is parity coverage when it comes to journalistic insight. We are currently in the build up to the British Lions v Kangaroos Test series; I just thought I would mention it because you would never know by reading either "The Guardian" or "The Observer". Yesterday's rugby league coverage in "The Observer" was 16 square cm, compared to two pages on rugby union.

This begs the questions, where were the interviews? Where were the insights into the shortcomings the Lions may face in vital areas due to injury? Where was the focus on the strength and weaknesses of the Australian side? In other words, where was the journalism in the lead up to next week's first Test? There has been little or no journalism to speak of, which considering the importance of the series for rugby league (Britain's second largest spectator sport after football) can only be described as disgraceful.

If this state of events were just a temporary situation, then I would not need to write this letter. Unfortunately for rugby league this is no short-term oversight, as a quick look at your coverage over the last 12 months will all too easily prove. Rugby league consistently gets starved of publicity in the national newspapers, denying the game any chance of credibility at a national level. We can now see the pages and pages of type devoted to recent union converts who have been playing at the highest level in league for years. Have they only just become quality players worthy of recognition? Of course not. It is only now that they have moved to union that the press will allow their skills to be appreciated on a national stage.

I have been impressed by the quality of league journalism in some of your competitors, "The Independent" in particular. Even when working in the south, as I frequently do, it still provides league coverage, unlike your southern editions. I find it sickening that the once "Manchester Guardian" can turn its back on rugby league and embrace the press apartheid system that "The Telegraph" and "The Times" newspapers have made their trademark.

I have read "The Guardian" since I was 16 years old and I do not want to stop buying this fine newspaper, but I will if this unjustifiable inequality is allowed to continue. I will give the paper three months to review its coverage and where I spend my money after that will depend on what action you decide to take. If you keep failing me and many other league fans in this country, then I will reluctantly switch to "The Independent", as I would never stoop to buy the "Daily Mail".

Please do not get the impression that I am anti rugby union, as I am not. I am just against the way the national press seems to think league is just there to be used as a whipping boy, despite the quality of the teams and players that demonstrate their skills week in and week out in Super League

Yours in sport

30,000 rugby league fans

APPENDIX 1

Rugby League Media Petition
Presentation Frontsheet

Mission Statement/Rationale

'We, the undersigned Rugby League Supporters, can accept constructive criticism by the media but deplore the constant trashing of
our chosen sport. Certain media outlets go way over the top and we
now feel enough is enough. We have the right to be treated with
respect in sport.

Whilst Rugby League clubs at amateur, semi professional, professional, student and armed forces levels are present in all counties of
England, Scotland, Ireland and Wales the myth that the sport is still
a northern regional one is perpetuated.

The perception by many thousands of rugby league fans is that
whilst regional printed media and broadcast serves the sport and its
followers well, media coverage on a national basis by newspapers and
broadcasters is:

* is disproportionately small compared to other sports covered
* superficial or plainly inaccurate in content
* frequently presented in disrespectful or mocking language

Uniquely, rugby league is frequently and routinely attacked by journalists of 'another sport', as if by agenda.

The right of reply is seldom, if ever, offered or acknowledged.

THE PETITION

'National' broadcasters present such television programmes as are made on a regional basis only.

Borne out of frustration and a sense of injustice, a petition was embarked on by individuals in an attempt to gauge the depth of public feeling, which spread through parts of the rugby league fraternity gaining its own momentum by volunteer effort.

By no means exhaustive and representing only a small sample of its potential, between 4th May 2001 and 24th November 2001, the total of signatures collected and hereby attached is 30,000

APPENDIX 2

Points arising from Media Petition:

1. Without any prompting many signatories stated that due to the paucity of RL coverage they no longer bought national, or in some cases, any newspapers.

2. Omly a few people disagreed with the petition, which amounted approximately 0.1% of those approached.

3. Very little 'anti-union' sentiment was expressed by signatories.

NB. Radio Leeds RU correspondent expressed disappointment at the coverage Rotherham RU had received in the national media during their Zurich Premiership season.

4. Geographical spread of signatories included Aberdeen, Bath, Cheltenham, Derby, Edinburgh, Fareham, Sunderland, Lincoln, Plymouth, Birmingham, Northampton, Southampton, Oxford, Chippenham, Luton, Wimbledon, Southend-on-Sea, Cardiff, Swansea, Belfast, Dublin etc. and many other countries (including Australia, USA, France, Switzerland, Holland, Russia, Malta and Canada.). Especially given the limited geographical spread of collectors, it would seem that far from being a parochial northern interest only, RL draws its support from all over the country.

5. Notable signatories include: -
* Lord Hoyle of Warrington
* Terry Wynn MEP
* David Hinchliffe MP
* Eddie Hemmings, Mike Stephenson, Phil Clarke (Sky Sports commentary team) and their producer Angela Powers.

THE PETITION

* The Head Coaches from Featherstone, St Helens, Wakefield, Oldham, Sheffield and Hull are known to have signed, as well as several players and ex-players from Warrington, Castleford, Hull, Wigan (including the legendary Billy Boston), Wakefield, St Helens, Oldham and Sheffield. Others may have signed and be amongst the many thousands of signatures.
* Various directors of London, Bradford, Huddersfield, Hunslet, Oldham, Gateshead and Whitehaven.
* Several national RL journalists.
* Referees and linesmen.

6. Known media outlets expressing support/publishing related material included: -

Sky Sports
GMR (Greater Manchester Radio)
North Cumberland Times & Star
Radio Humberside
St Helens Reporter
Radio Leeds
The Independent
Radio Merseyside
Hull Daily Mail
WIRE FM (Warrington)
Liverpool Echo
WISH FM (St Helens and Wigan)
Widnes Weekly
Warrington Guardian
Various internet sites
Yorkshire Evening Post

7. When advised of this petition's existence, the response received from national newspapers and broadcasters seemed ambivalent, intransigent and generally unaware or unconcerned as to the grievance that this exercise demonstrates.

THE PETITION

We the undersigned Rugby League Supporters, can accept constructive criticism by the media but deplore the constant trashing of our chosen sport. Certain media outlets go way over the top and we now feel enough is enough. We have the right to be treated with respect in sport.

Name	Signed	Town/City
IAN BELL		WARRINGTON
DONNA IRVING	D Irving	BRADFORD
NEIL TAYLOR	N Taylor	NEWCASTLE
WAYNE PENSON		Hertford
M PENSON		
J. Rolofe		Lyon
LOIS METCALFE	LMetcalfe	Ripon
MATTHEW MORTON	Matthew Morton	Ripon
Sarah Mockley		Durham
John Spell		Leeds
Michael Sullivan		Nottingham
Esther Bilby	E Bilby	Cambridge
Danny Williams		Cambridge
V WALTON	V Walton	LIVERPOOL
J. LOCKWOOD		BRADFORD
Claire Rushford		Bradford
N. Stephenson	N Stephenson	Huddersfield
Maureen Lyons	Maureen Lyons	BRADFORD
L. HOPKINSON		BRADFORD
W.A. WHALLEY	W.A. Whalley	WARRINGTON
D WYNN		WIGAN
F ALLISON		OXFORD CAVALIERS
P BENSON		DRIGHLINGTON W. YORKS
S. Cogwell		Manchester
Niel Wood		Rochdale
MARY SHIRES	M Shires	DEWSBURY
C. S. WALTON		LEEDS
T. N. WALTON	T N Walton	LEEDS
P. SLATER	P Slater	CUMBRIA
K Butcher		''
C. Parrington		''
I DIXON		''

THE PETITION

APPENDIX 3

Resources Used

As an amateur, unsponsored and spontaneous 'fans' initiative the petition was started with: -

No media contacts and limited experience

No personnel - voluntary effort was picked up along the way

No budget for stationery, postage, travel, advertising etc

Signatories were collected by ad-hoc volunteer effort in their own spare time as convenient and practical as possible.

Given the relatively uncoordinated and sporadic nature of the initiative, the large majority of potential signatories will not be aware of the petition's existence, or would be unlikely to come into contact with any of the relatively few collectors, or have access to the internet petition. The initiative should therefore be considered by no means exhaustive and represents only a small sample of its potential.

APPENDIX 4

Presentation

It is intended that this petition and/or this attachment be presented to: -

Parliamentary RL Group - c/o David Hinchliffe MP (Wakefield)
Press Complaints Commission
National newspaper Editors and Sports Editors
BBC Television
BBC Radio 5 Live
TalkSport
Rugby Football League
Super League (Europe)
Sky Sports
Rugby League Supporters Association
Local newspapers and radio
Rugby League newspapers and magazines

APPENDIX 5

The following people subscribed to this book:

ABERDEEN
Phil Stockton

BILLINGE, UPHOLLAND & GARSWOOD
John & Eileen Taylor
Arthur & Margaret Makin
Nigel & Edna Deakin
Brian Duffy
Gill & Joan Cross
Graham & Shirley Morris
Derek & Julie White
Jim & Margaret Diffley
Pam & John Turner
Angela Mullen
Frank & Freda Woods
Brian & Sandra Davies
Maurice Gaskill
John & Marjorie Shufflebottom
Andy & Christine Hamilton
Luke Hamilton
Bernard Higham
Wendy Neal
George & Chris Wiswell
John & Margaret McDonald
Arthur & Brenda Keir

BRADFORD, SHIPLEY & BATLEY
Steve Murphy
Phil & Linda Oates
Laurie & Lynne Hopkinson
Sal Hopkinson
Geoff Lee
Andrew Foster
Stuart Duffy BULLS
Michael Stephenson
Lee Carson

BOLTON
Peter & Vera Gregory
Brian & Margaret Greaves

BRISBANE, AUSTRALIA
Bill Abernethy

BRISTOL
Phil Cole

Co ANTRIM, CONWY, CORNWALL & CARDIFF
Ray & Kathleen McCormick
Harry & Mamie Gent
Alan & Elaine Naughton
Dr. Jack Whittaker MP FRCP
John & Christine Middleton

DONCASTER & DURHAM
David Priestley
Adrian & Katherine Lodge

FEATHERSTONE, WAKEFIELD & PONTEFRACT
John & Michelle Hanvey
Richard Shaw-Wright
Mick Hartley
Stephen Parker
Ian & Angela Hague
Peter Bell
Amanda Mason

FRANCE
John Marchant

HALIFAX & YORK
S Evans York RL Historian
Paul & Joseph Boyne
Tony Ackroyd

THE PETITION

GOMERSAL YORKS
Peter Benson Drighlington RLFC

HARTLEPOOL & HULL
Donald & June Marshall
Neil Williamson
Chris Turner
Shane & Kim Richardson
from Carol, Steve & Chris
Shaun French
Zoe Booth

ILFORD, ESSEX
Lloyd Anderson

KENDAL
Shaun McMullen

LANCASTER, CLITHEROE & LYTHAM ST ANNES
Richard De-La-Riverie
John Thomason
Nic Etchells-Skeat
Andy & Sam Mullaney

LIVERPOOL, WIRRAL, SOUTH-PORT & ORMSKIRK
Stephen & Lisa Davies
Thomas Patterson
Phil Speakman
John Wilson
Irene Wignall
Phil Watkinson
Eric & Beryl Bond
George & Eileen Samuels
Carl Davies
Bob Murray
Andy & Laura Murray

LONDON
South London Storm RLFC

MANCHESTER, LEEDS, SWINTON & WILMSLOW
Allen & Anne Worthington
Geoff Wilkinson
Mick Penn
Stephen Johnson
Cliff Spracklen RLSA
Richard & Sue Malone

NORLEY, CHESHIRE
David & Pauline Glenn

ROCHDALE
Mark Wynn fabrications

SOLIHULL, BROMSGROVE, TELFORD & LEICESTER
Darren Broadhurst
John & Ali Fairhurst
Joyce Smith
George & Linda Jones
Mick Dyer Chairman M

ST. HELENS
Michael Campbell (Wire)
Pie Magic a true Saint
Roger & Ann Grime
Keith & Pam Taylor
Paul & Pat Greenall
Bernard & Lynn Smith
Michael & Hazel Hendriksen
Joe & Maureen Woods
Eric & Marjorie Gent
Russel & Lynn Gent
Brian & Shirley Cross
Ken & Pauline Harding
Olive Gent
Keith & Wendy Hale
Michael Keating
Stephen & Clare Pickavance
David & Paula Gent
Sam & Lynn Howard
Dave & Sylvia Barnett
Andrew Barnet

THE PETITION

Charlie Featherstone
Mary Appleton
Paul Appleton
Andrew & Margaret Appleton
Graham & Jacqueline Innes
Linda & Ste Pownall
Dave & Karen Abbott
Hannah Molyneux
Shiela Cheyne
Sandra McCormick
Nora Robinson
Marlene Downey
Paul Grime
John Grime
Michael Grime
Aidan Shukie
John & Phylis Holmes
Dave Dooley
Les & Marjorie Wilson
I'm Webbo!!
Alex & Judith Service
Glen 'Bumper' Dwyer
Kate & Jack Leivesley
Nick Gribben
Keiron & Cath Traynor
Dave & Rita Molyneux
Brian & Jean Challinor
Alan Gordon
Ron, Ivy & Sue Sumner
Linda & John junior Dotters
Shaun & Pat Kilgallon
Tex & Sandra Martindale
Kerry Walmsley
Dave & Sue Welling
Clive & Rose Briscoe
Ashley Rankin
Lianne Rankin
Harry Gee
Tom & Julia Wood
Andy Lea
Neville & Linda Bond
Simon & Debora Speight
Helen & John Atherton
Stew Whitefield

Joanne Whitfield
Geoff & Sue Sarsfield
Carla Doran
Stan & Sue Hill
Dave & Barbara Jones
Peter Donaldson
Ste & Sue Winstanley
Phil & Pat Carlin
Michael & Leonnie Hough
Andrew Critchley
David Lyon (British Bronco)

SUTTON, SURREY
Michael Wall

WIGAN
Denis & Margaret Slater
Dave & Sue Wilkinson
John & Mary Smethurst
Terry Wynn MEP
Doris Wynn
Dennis & Val Houghton
John & Angela Hulstrom
Michelle & Natalie Johnson
Billy & Dorothy Jones
Jack & Alice Taylor
Phil & Marian Brown
Brian & Shirley Cobourne
Alan & Ann Wilson
John & Sandra Flanagan
Tom & Barbara Woodward
Sam & Pat Blackledge
Joe & Karen Fairhurst
Roy & Barbara Ganderton
Joe & Mary Grindley
Howarth Johnson
Tom Ball
Ste & Sandra McDermott
Tom & Jean Gibbs
Barry & Sue Bridge
John & Norma Scott
Denis & Linda Marsden
Fred & Molly Welsby
Albi & Ann Shields

THE PETITION

Bob & Anita Murray
Ray & Maureen Green
Joe Marcroft
Peter & Betty Southworth
John & Lynsey Smith
Chris & Susan king
Fred & Beatrice Halliwell
Janice Johnson
Shane Wilson
Tony Higham
Ken & Wendy Kay
James & Barbara Read
Garvin & Geraldine Graves
Mark Woods
Jane Rawlinson
Mark & Karen Witherington
Martin Alcock
Gill Brown
Terry & Anne McNamee
John & Barbara McEnnaney
David & Susan Sixsmith
Michael & Clair Flanagan

WARRINGTON & WIDNES

John A Mitchell jonnysaint
Carl & Ben Porter
Barry & Kate Robinson
Lee & Sam Gent
George & Gillian Johnson
Phil Ward
Richard & Wandee Faulkner
Graham & Bradley Haynes

PLYMOUTH & MAIDENHEAD

Chris, Laura & Jack Moore
Kieron Lattimer